In memory of those brave men and women who gave their lives to keep peace and make this world a better place to live. NO MORE WARS!!

WORLD WAR 1
ADULT COLORING BOOK

An Artistic Coloring Book

By Edgar Fernandez

World War 1 - Adult Coloring Book

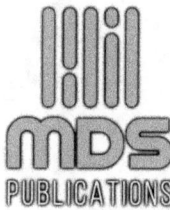

Design
MDS Publications 2018
www.mdspublications.com

Author
Edgar Fernandez

Cover Design
Edgar Fernandez

ISBN-13: **978-1984182487**
ISBN-10: **198418248X**

WORLD WAR I
ADULT COLORING BOOK

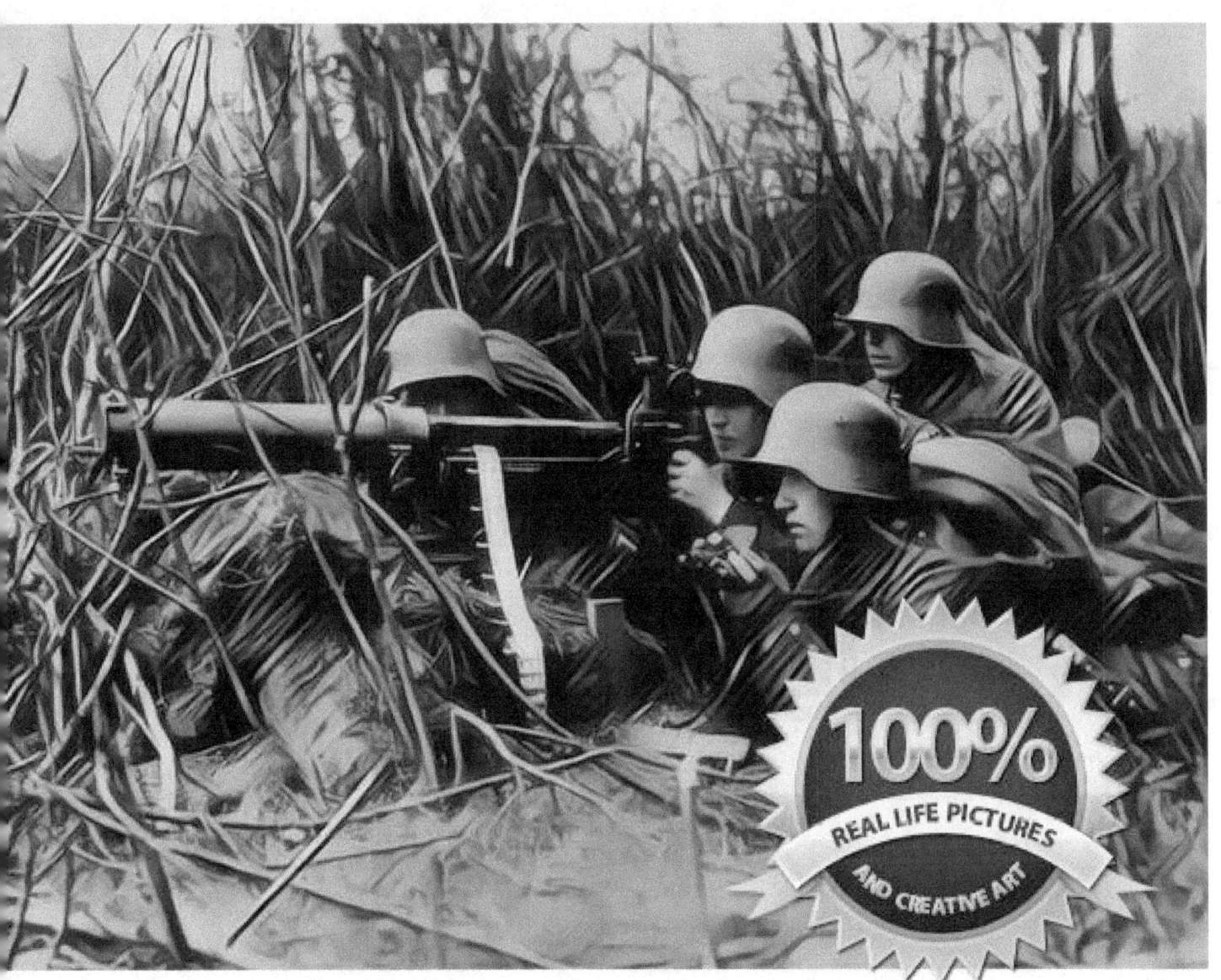

100%
REAL LIFE PICTURES
AND CREATIVE ART

An Artistic Coloring Book

By Edgar Fernandez

LIVE - LOVE - DREAM - WORK HARD - TRAIN HARD
YOU ONLY HAVE ONE LIFE

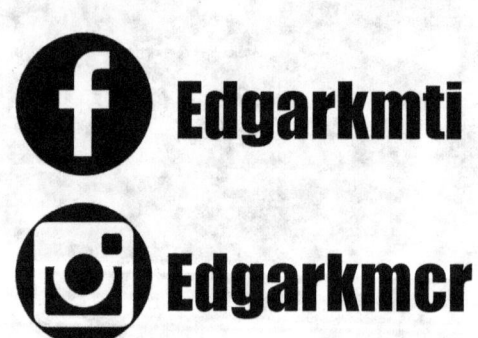

Edgarkmti

Edgarkmcr

Use this section to express yourself. What are your feelings about this picture?
What are your goals for today? What can you achieve today? Any new ideas?
Or just use this page to relax and draw something new.

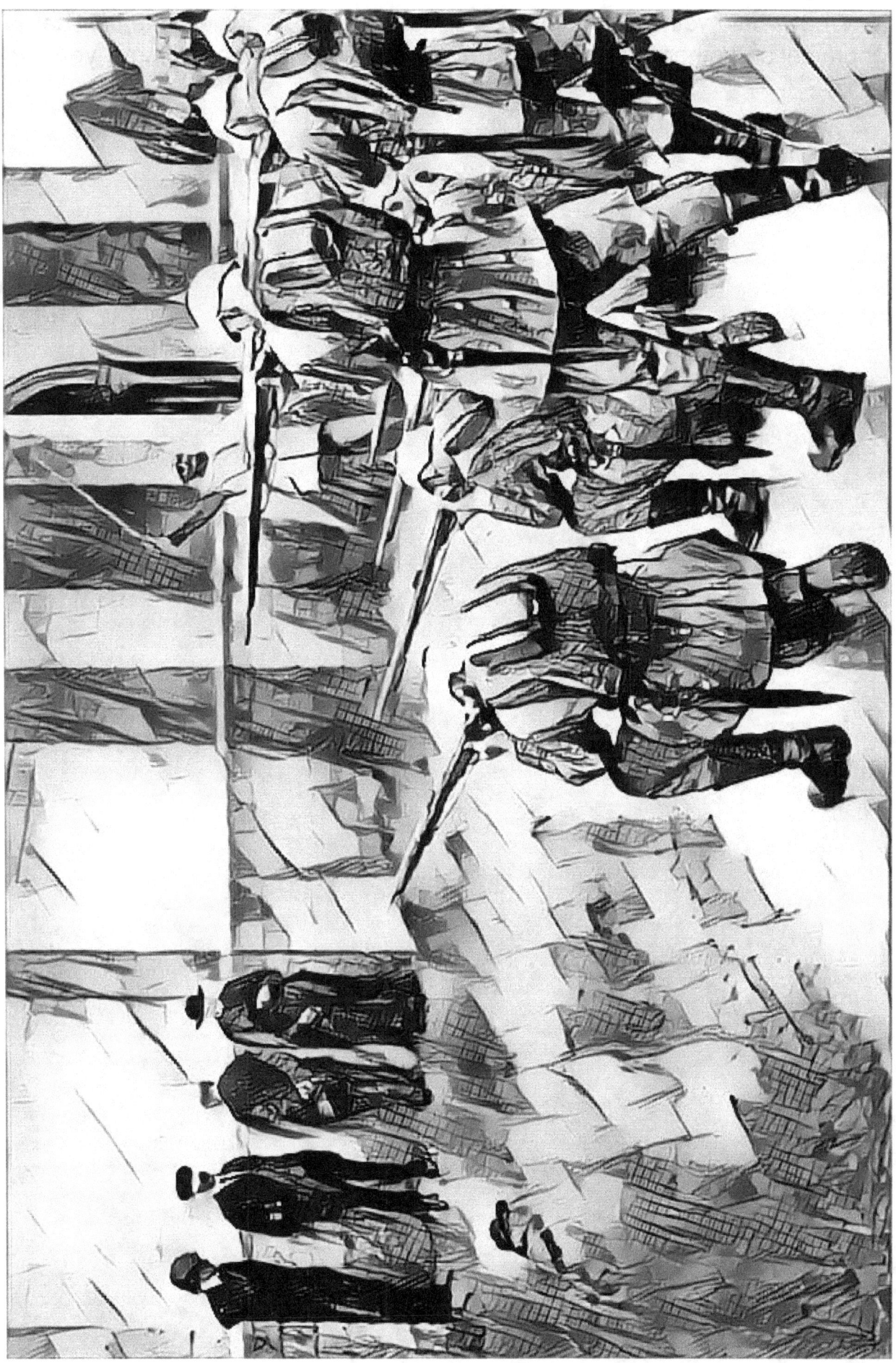

What would you do to stop war around the world. Consider the political, economical and other factors to create your solution. You never know, you can be the ONE!!

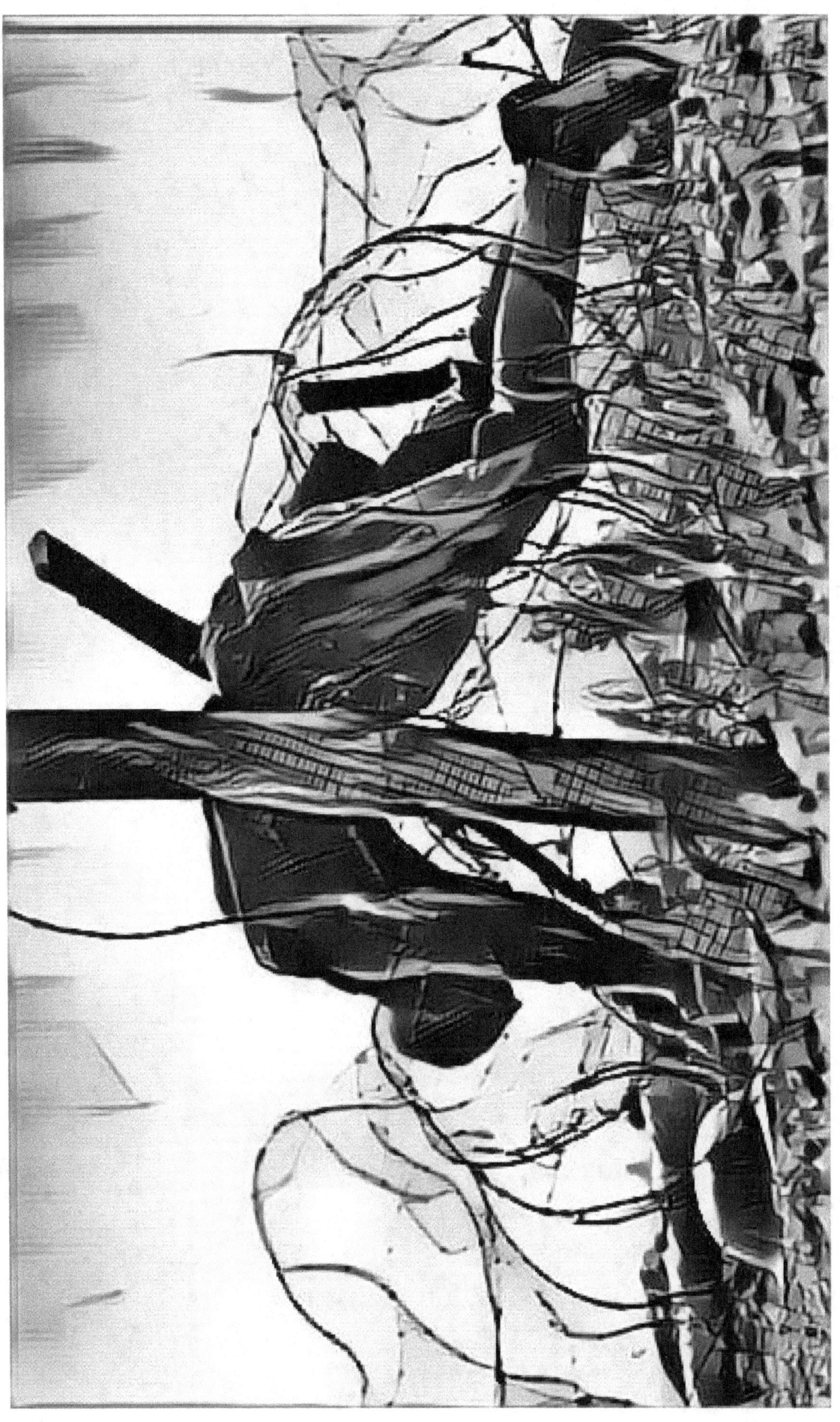

How confident are you actually? Tell me a story of your live when you achieve to overcome fear in other to do something. You might surprise
HOW STRONG YOU REALLY ARE!!

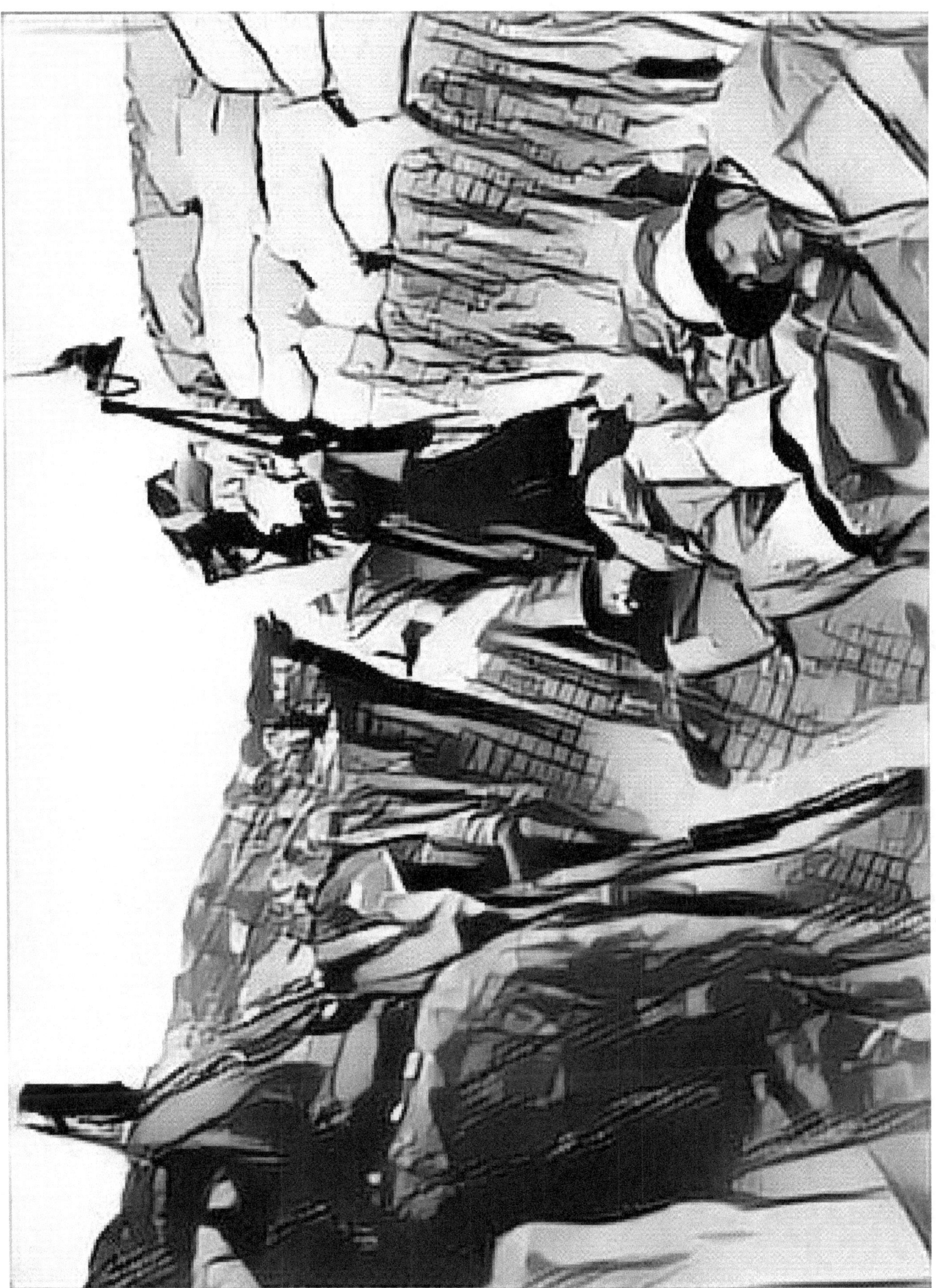

Have you ever participated in a parade? What was your role? If not, have you met someone who has participated in one?

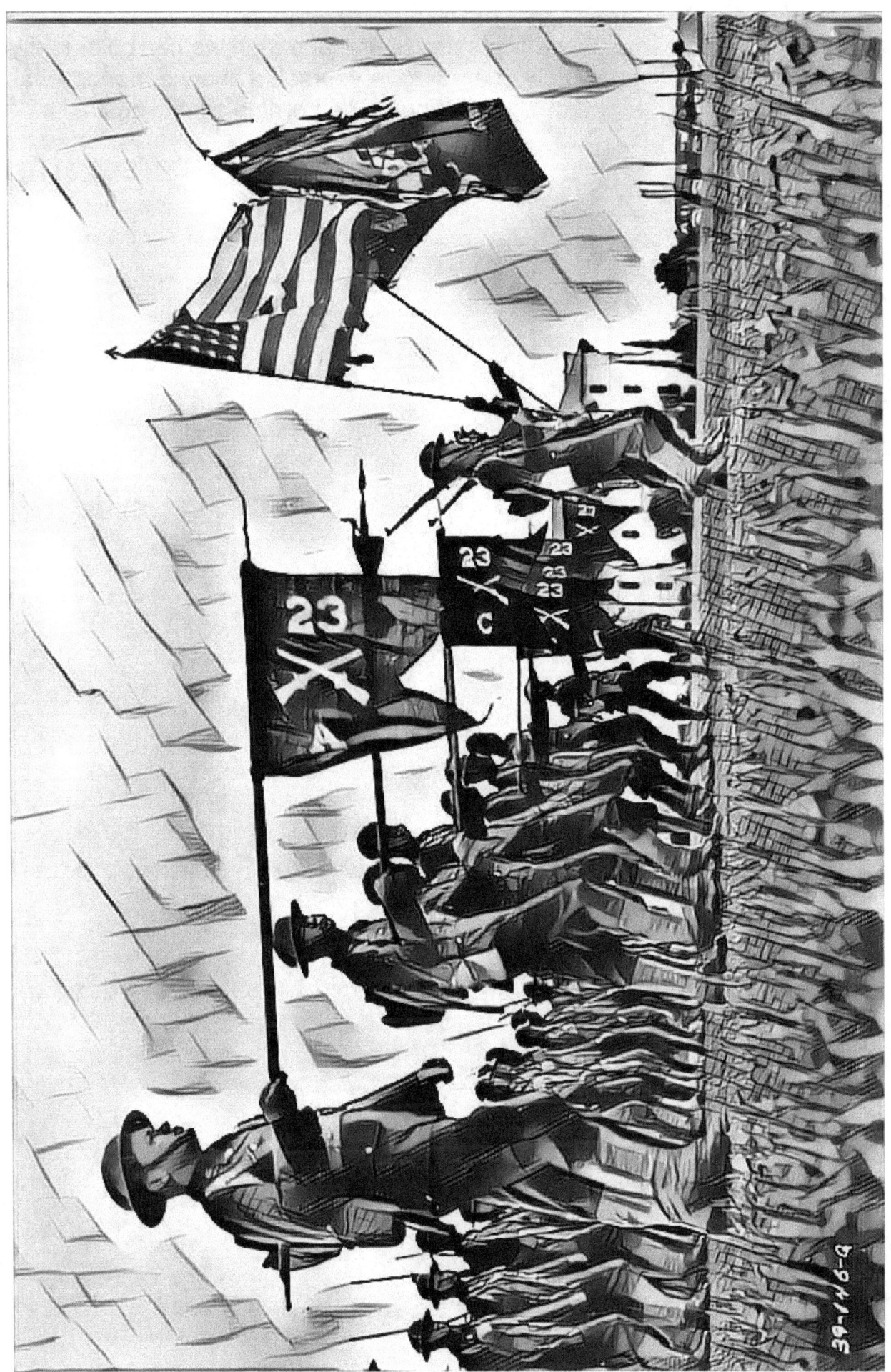

ok, let's try to draw what these pilots are seeing and then we can color it. If you think that you do not know how to draw, give yourself a chance, nobody was a great painter without first having made horrible scribblings.

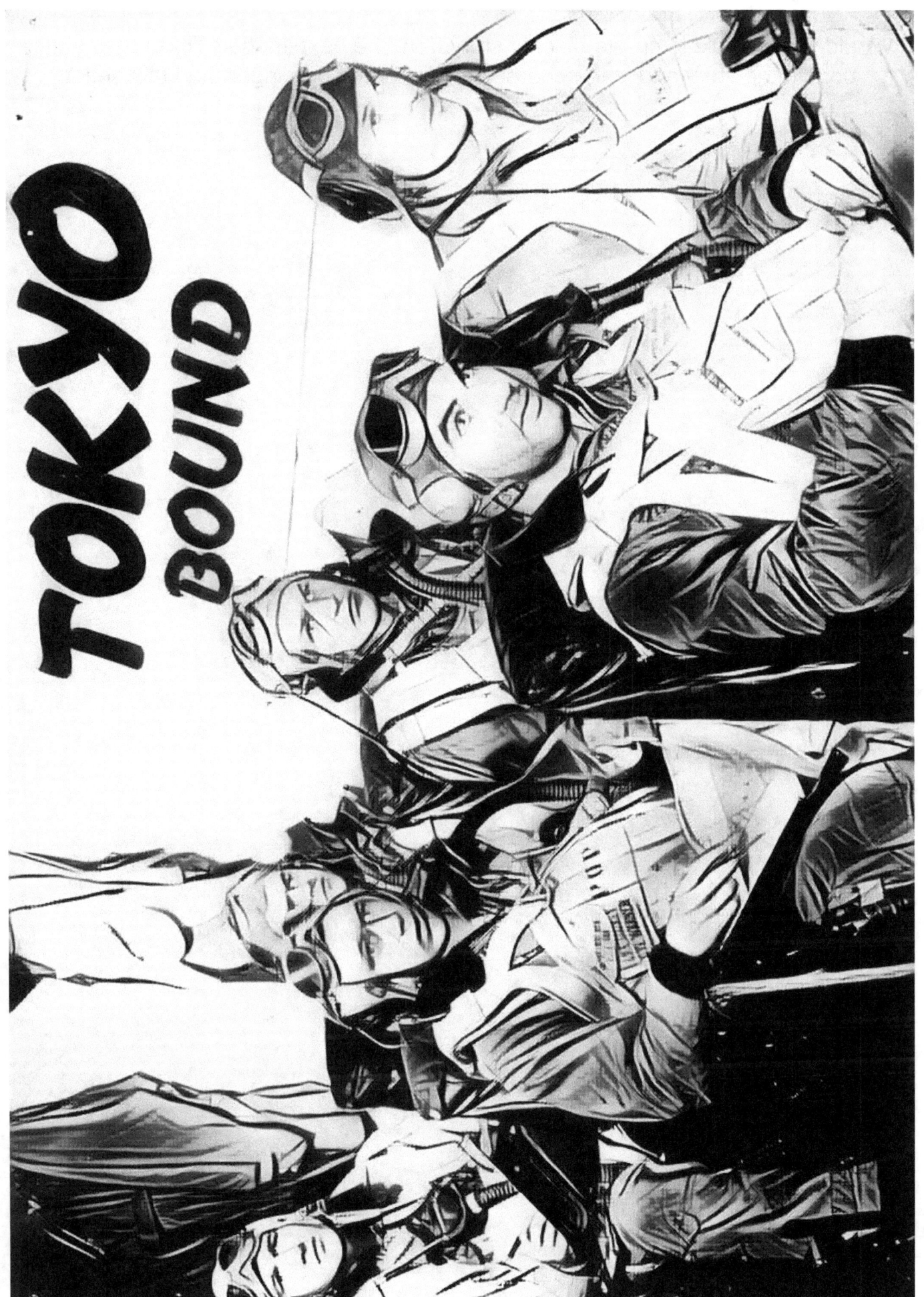

Would you be able to create a scary story from the next image? Try to be creative both in the story and in the characters. Try not to go bigger than this sheet.

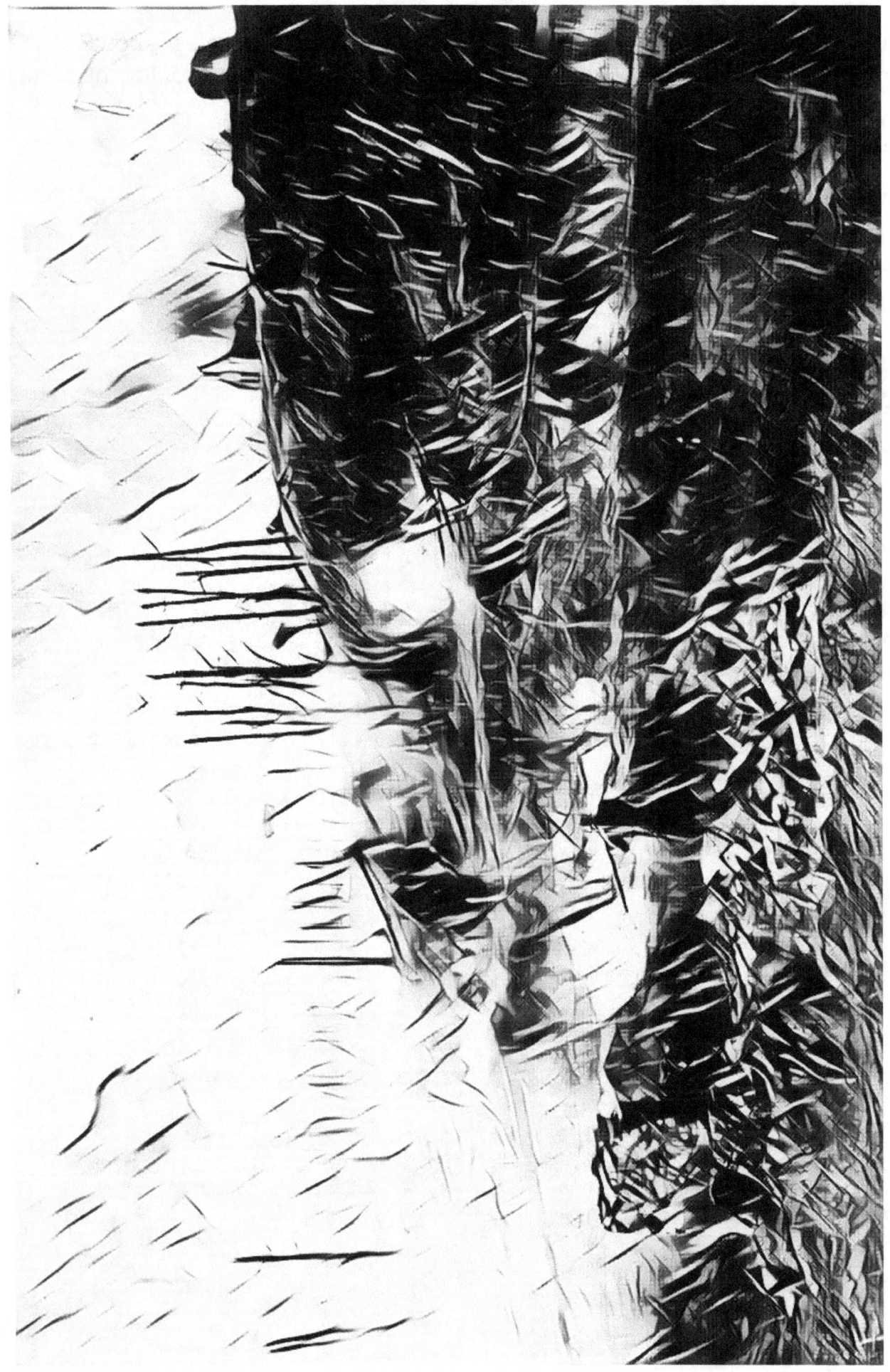

Have you ever participated in a protest? If so, what was the protest about? Something interesting happened? Create your story and take advantage of the inspiration.

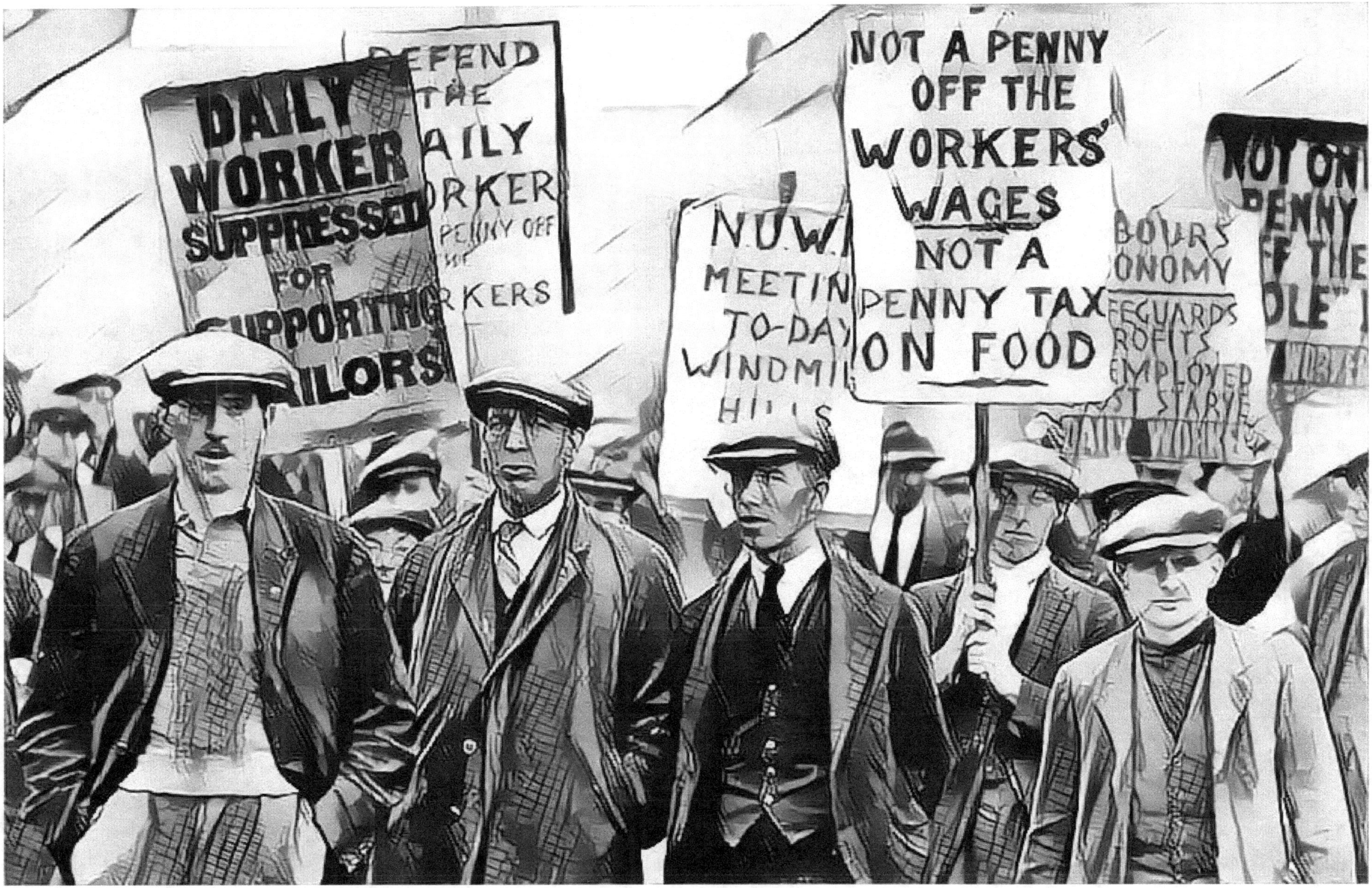
DAILY WORKER SUPPRESSED FOR
NOT A PENNY OFF THE WORKERS' WAGES NOT A PENNY TAX ON FOOD
MEETIN
TO-DAY

Create a short story with this picture. What can they be planning? What conversation can be going on? Don´t forget the names of your characters. Now color according to your story and mood of your characters.

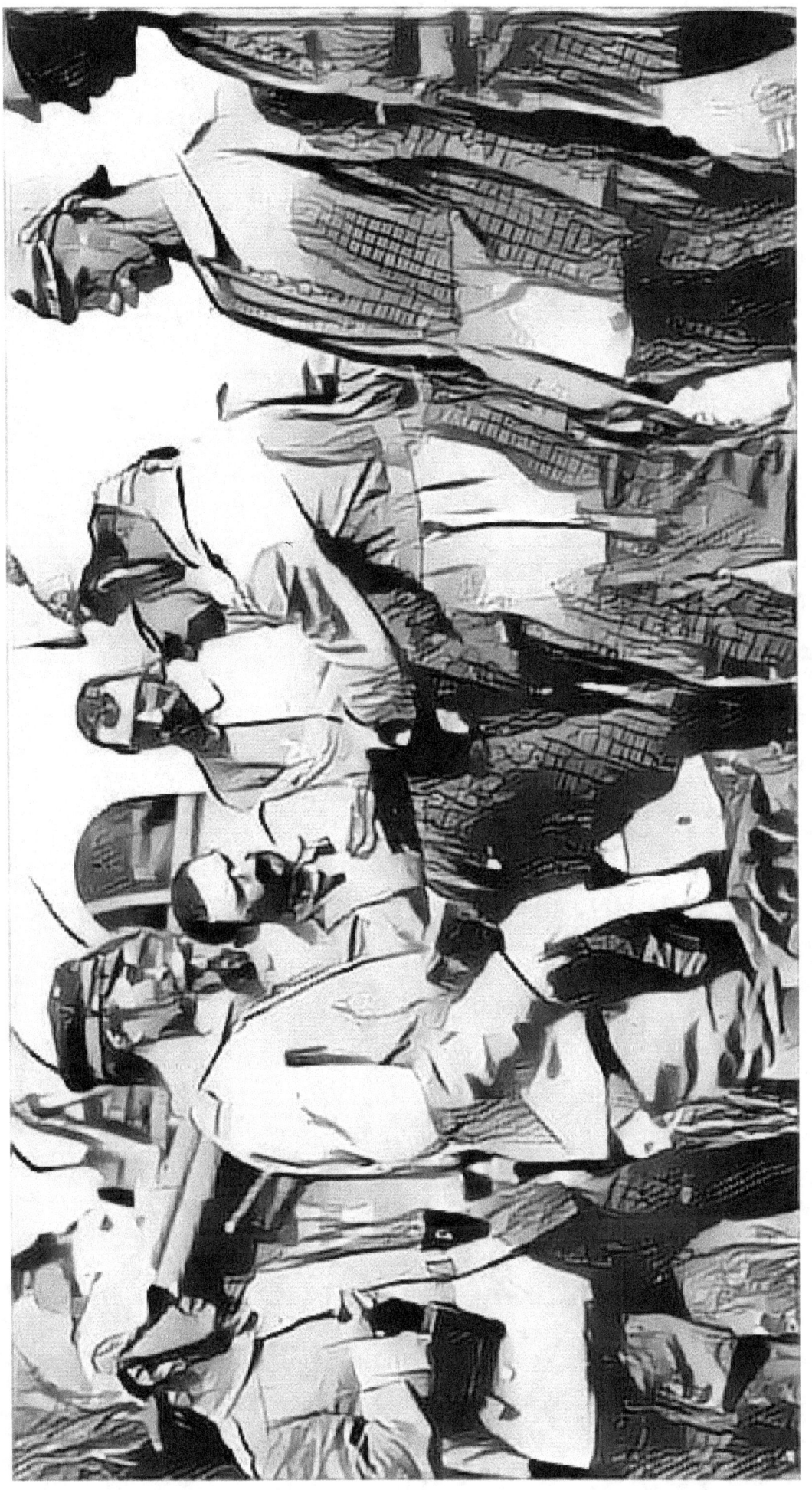

Have you ever been so tired that you fell deeply asleep in some uncomfortable place?
Tell your story and draw some images about it.

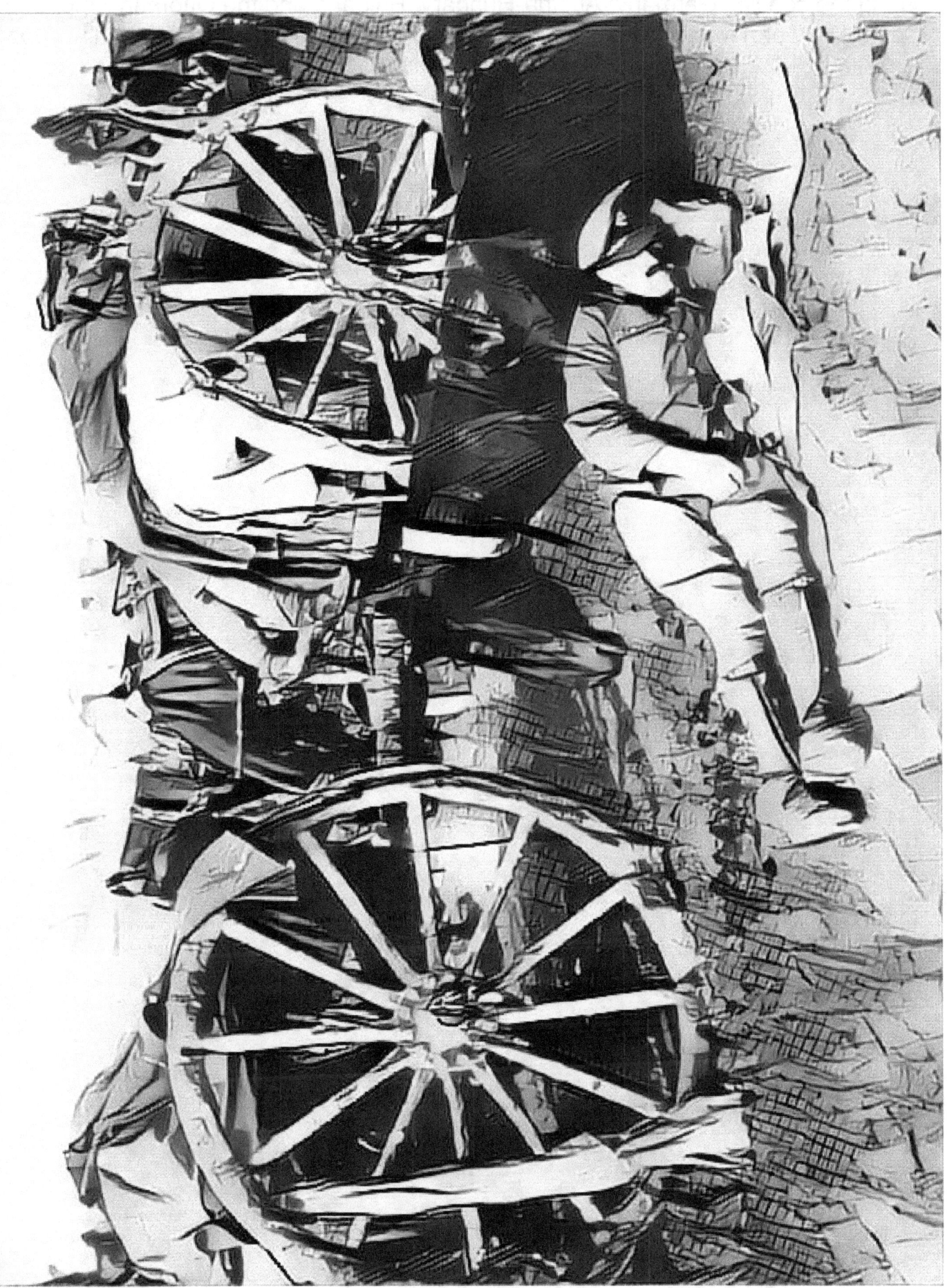

During the conflict, Germany, Austria-Hungary, Bulgaria and the Ottoman Empire (the Central Powers) fought against Great Britain, France, Russia, Italy, Romania, Japan and the United States (the Allied Powers).

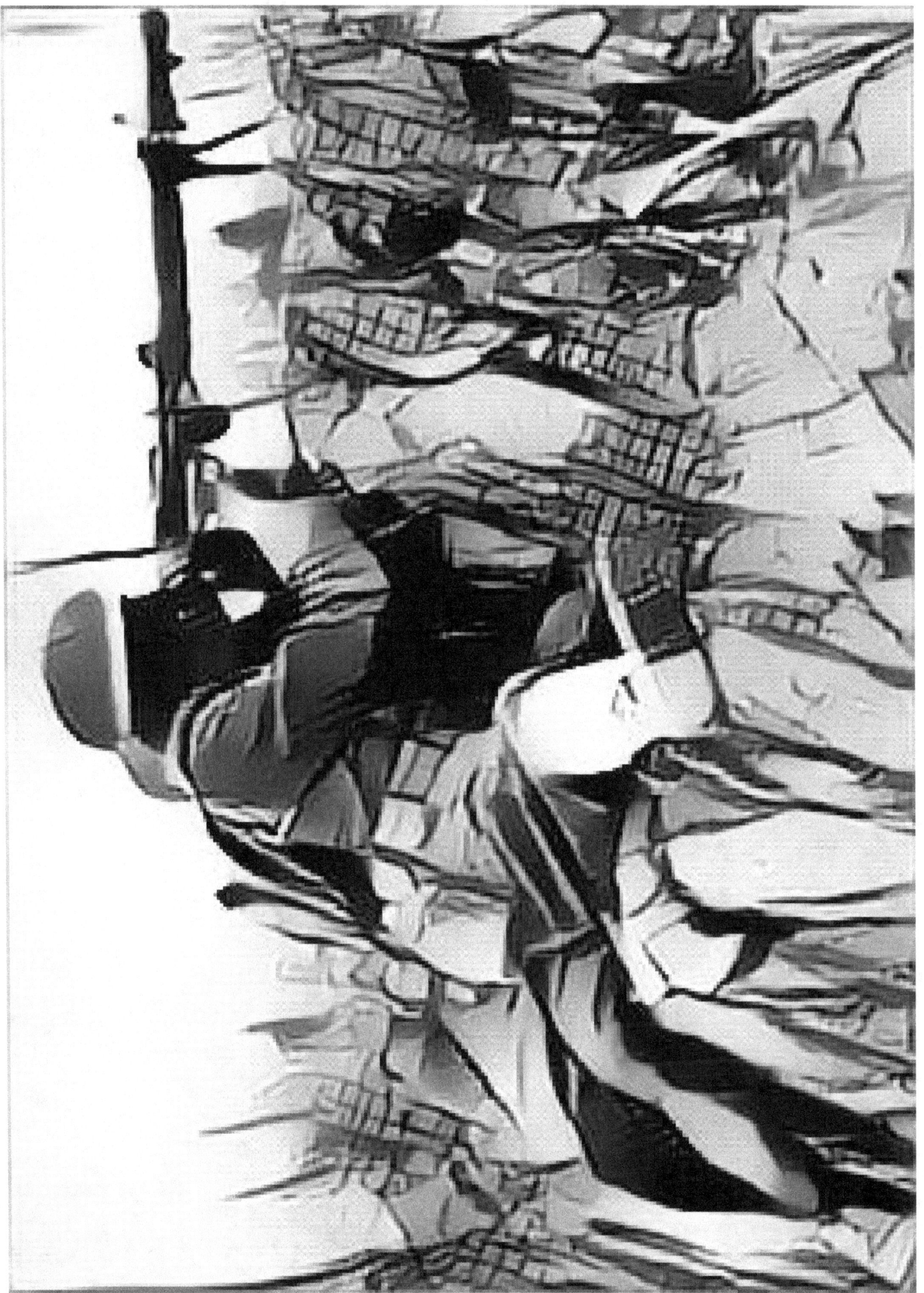

"I have no idea what we are still fighting for anyway, maybe because the newspapers portray everything about the war in a false light which has nothing to do with the reality.....There could be no greater misery in the enemy country and at home. The people who still support the war haven't got a clue about anything...If I stay alive, I will make these things public...We all want peace...What is the point of conquering half of the world, when we have to sacrifice all our strength?..You out there, just champion peace! ... We give away all our worldly possessions and even our freedom. Our only goal is to be with our wife and children again," Anonymous Bavarian soldier, 17 October 1914.

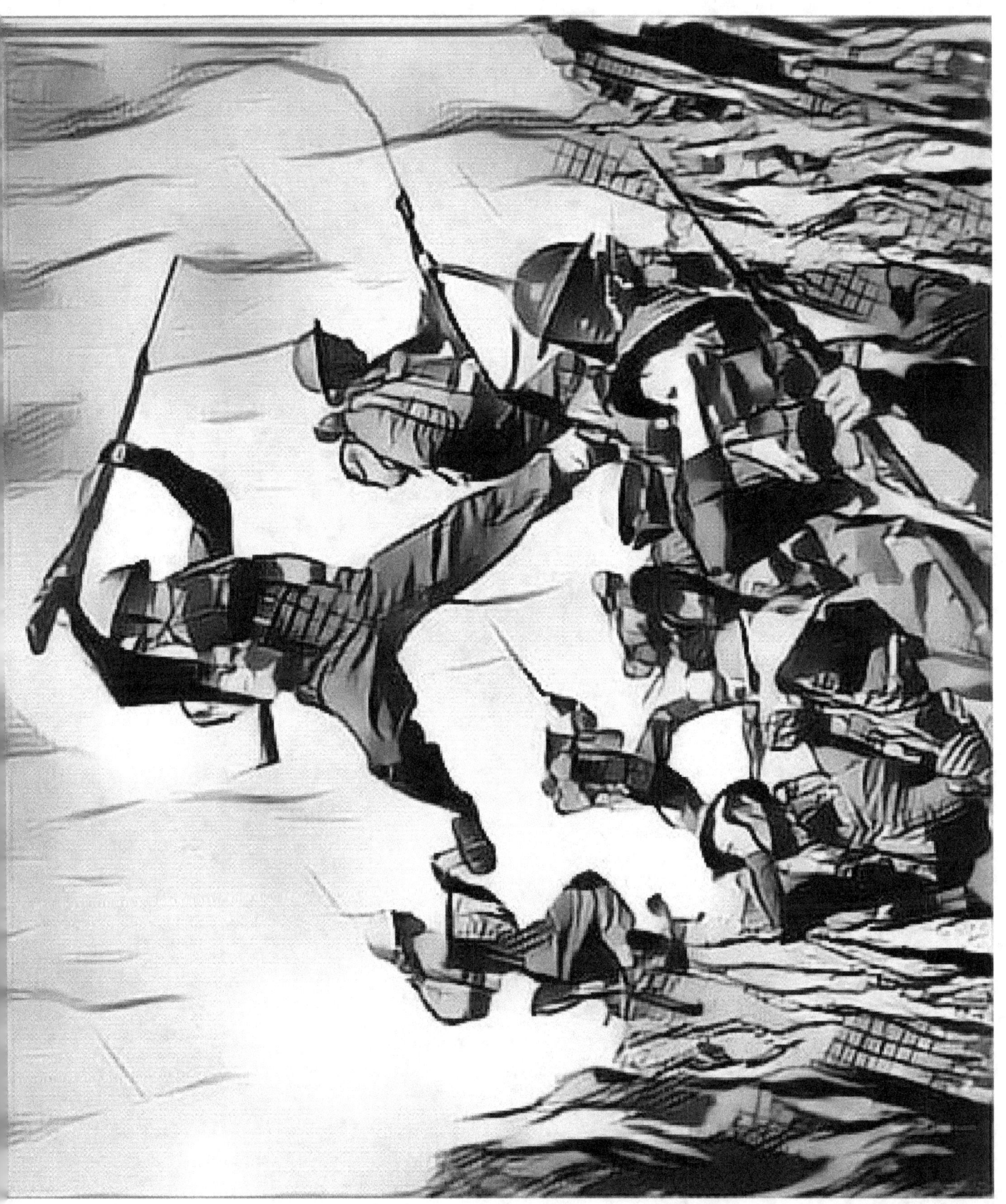

World War I was also known as the Great War, the World War, the War of the Nations, and the War to End All Wars.

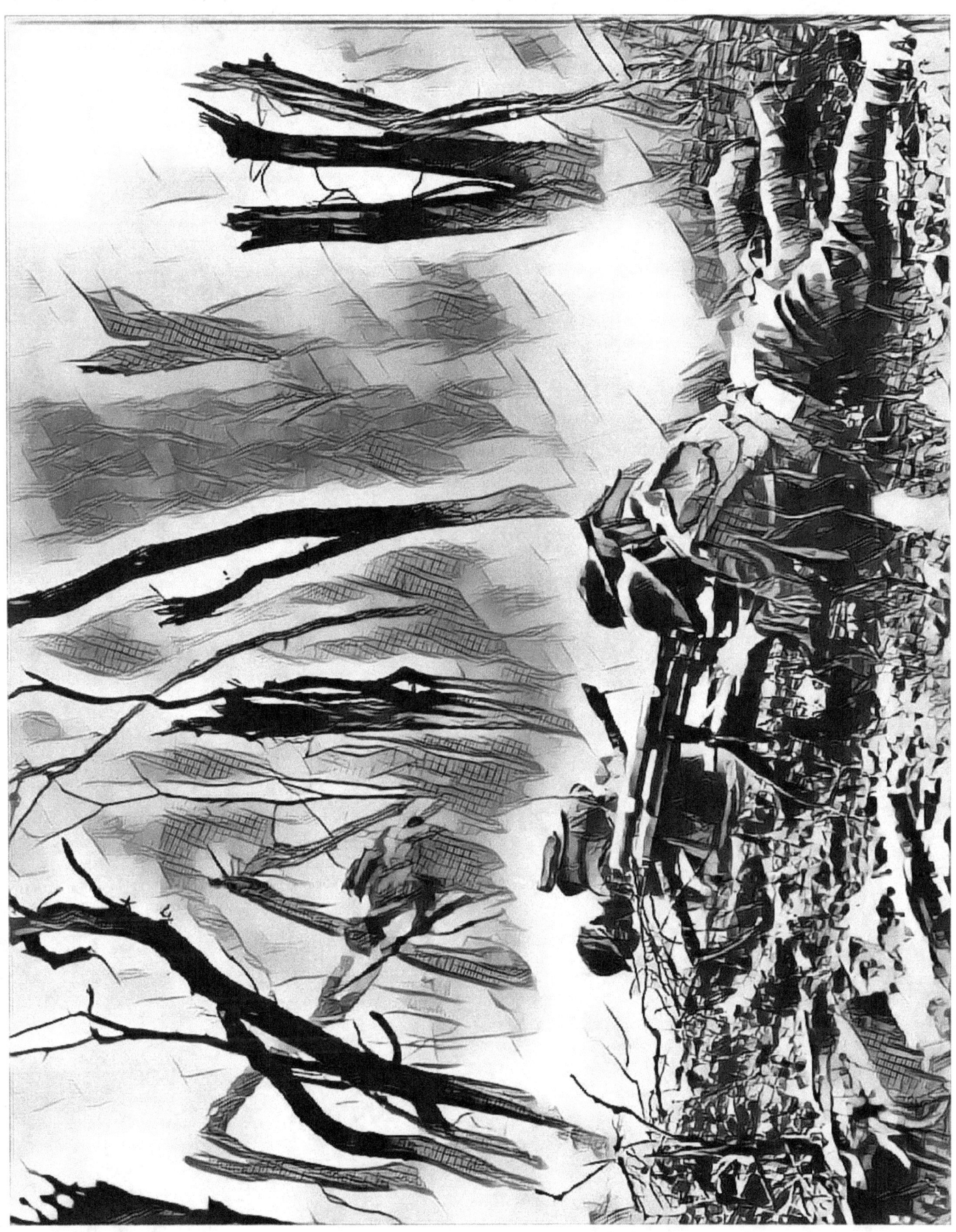

More than 65 million men from 30 countries fought in WWI. Nearly 10 million died. The Allies (The Entente Powers) lost about 6 million soldiers. The Central Powers lost about 4 million.

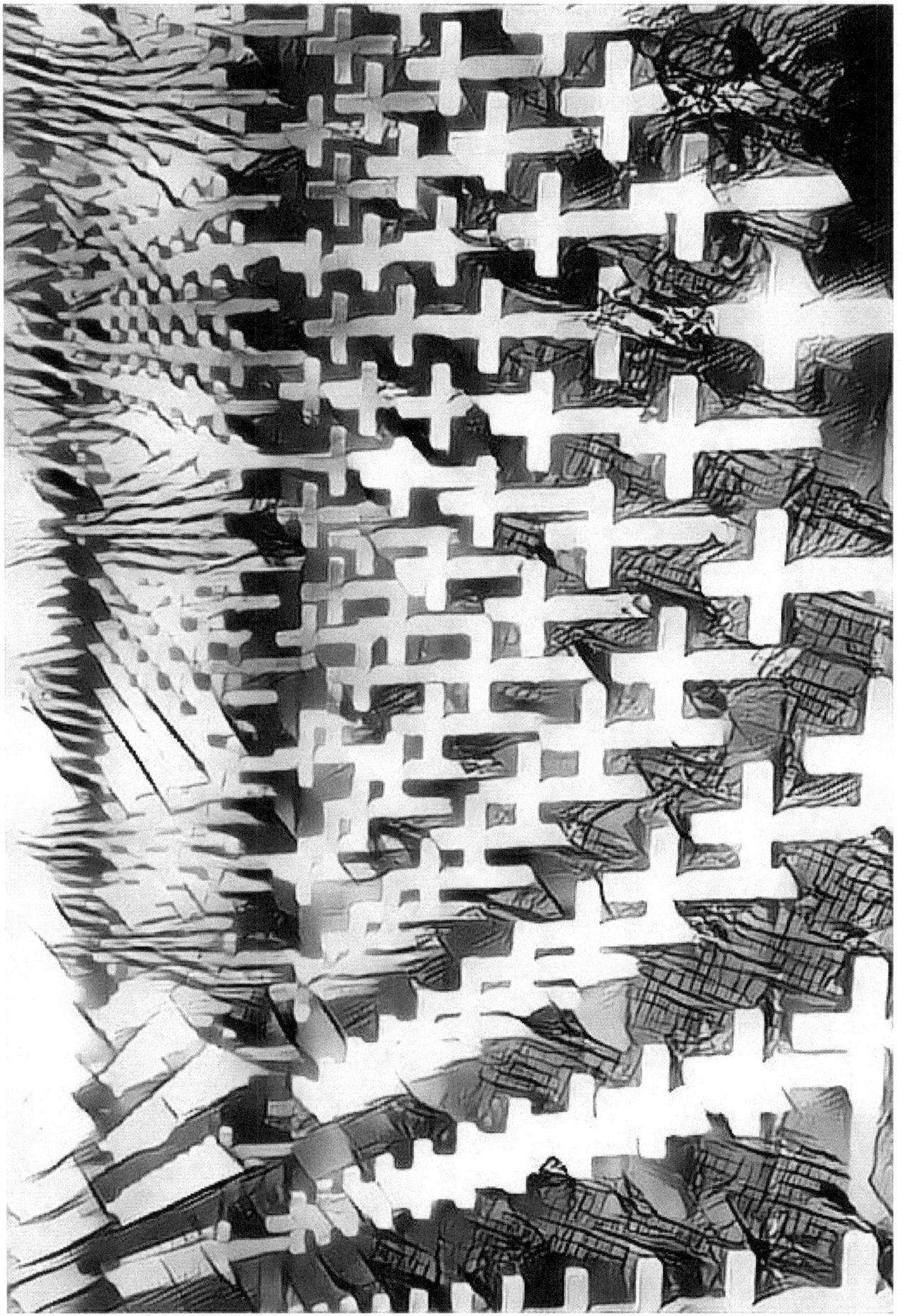

Approximately 30 different poisonous gases were used during WWI. Soldiers were told to hold a urine-soaked cloth over their faces in an emergency. By 1918, gas masks with filter respirators usually provided effective protection. At the end of the war, many countries signed treaties outlawing chemical weapons.

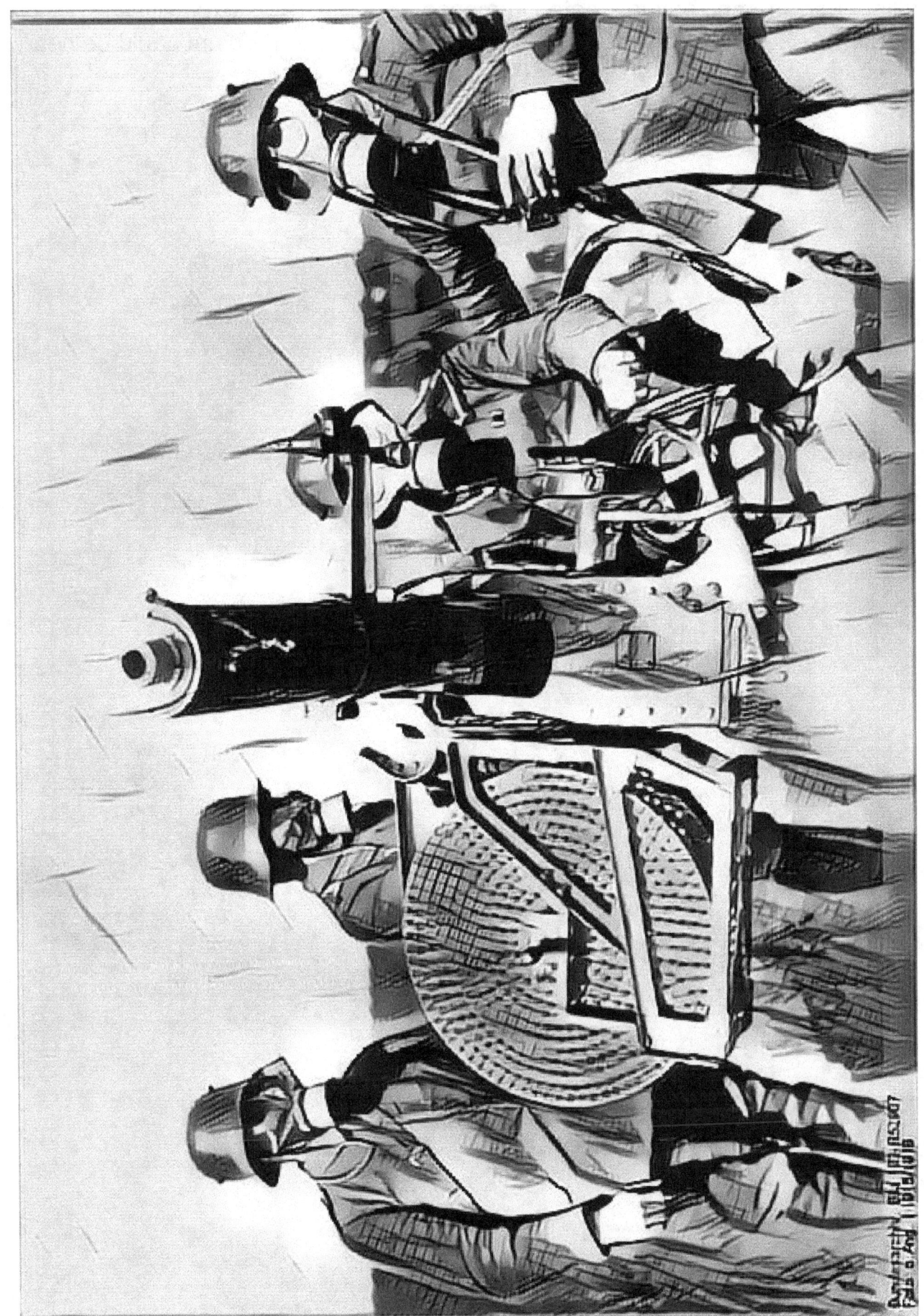

Artillery barrage and mines created immense noise. In 1917, explosives blowing up beneath the German lines on Messines Ridge at Ypres in Belgium could be heard in London 140 miles (220 km) away

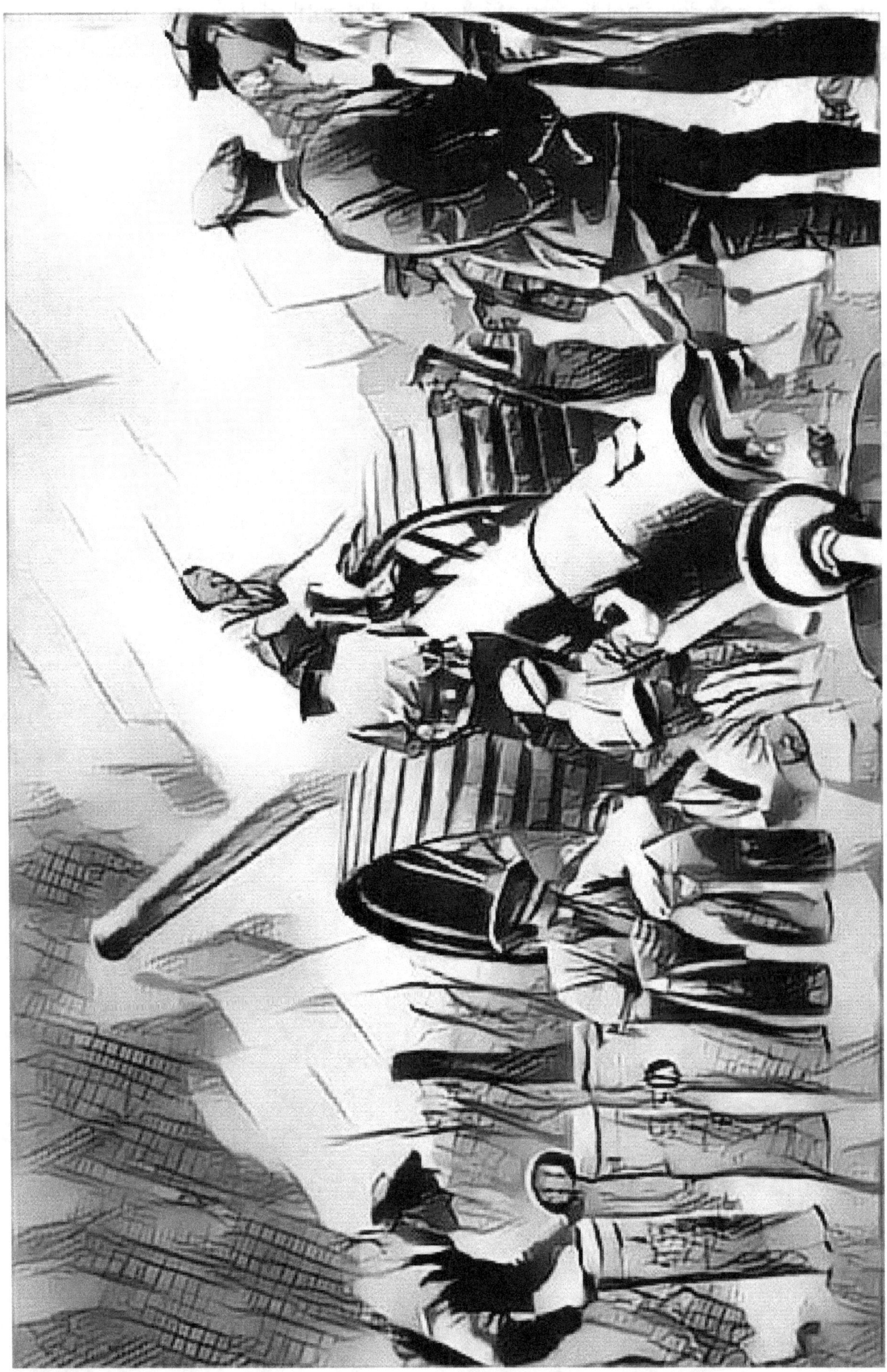

The war left thousands of soldiers disfigured and disabled. Reconstructive surgery was used to repair facial damage, but masks were also used to cover the most horrific disfigurement. Some soldiers stayed in nursing homes their entire lives.

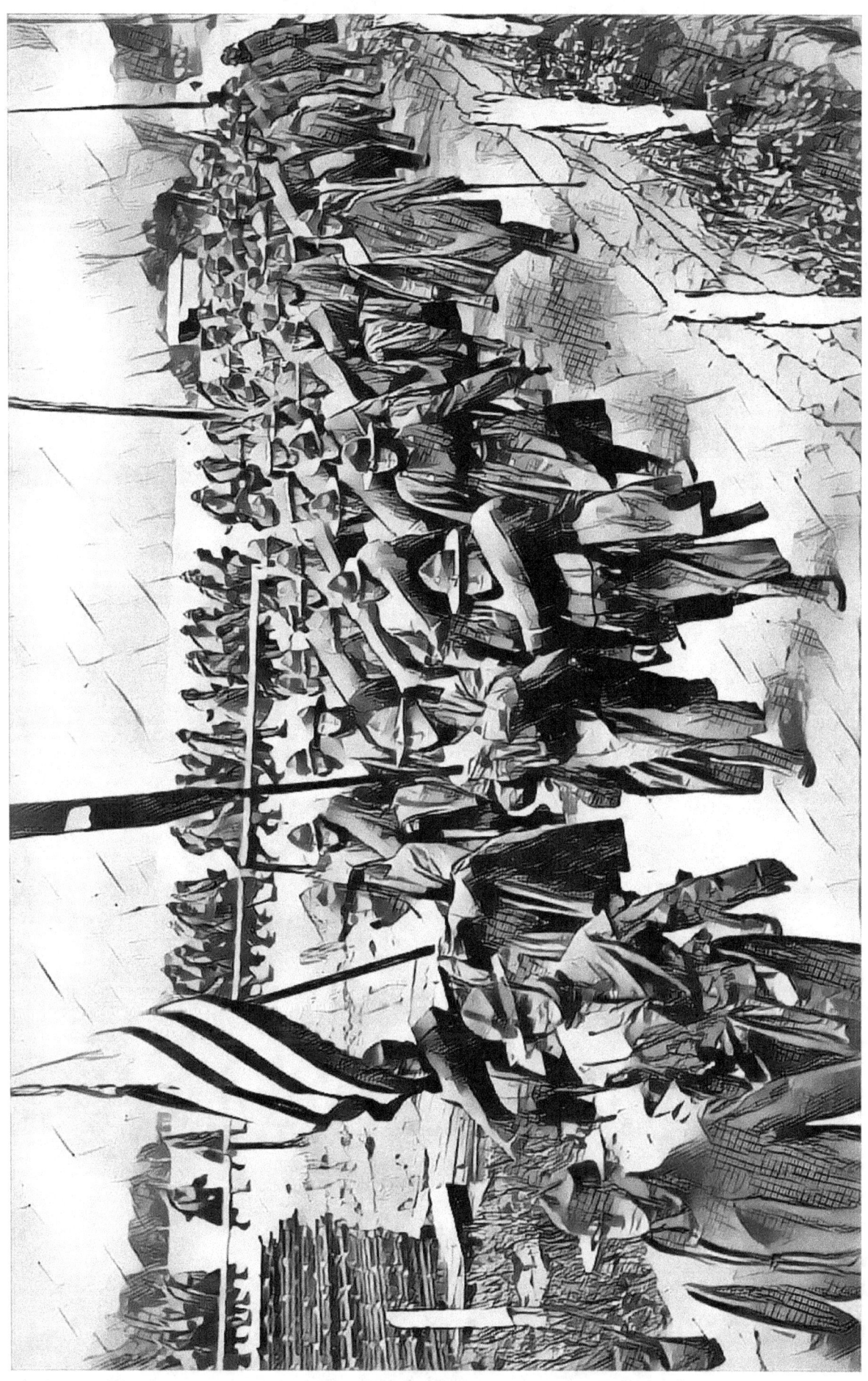

Imagine being this character. Tell your story and draw a map of the place.

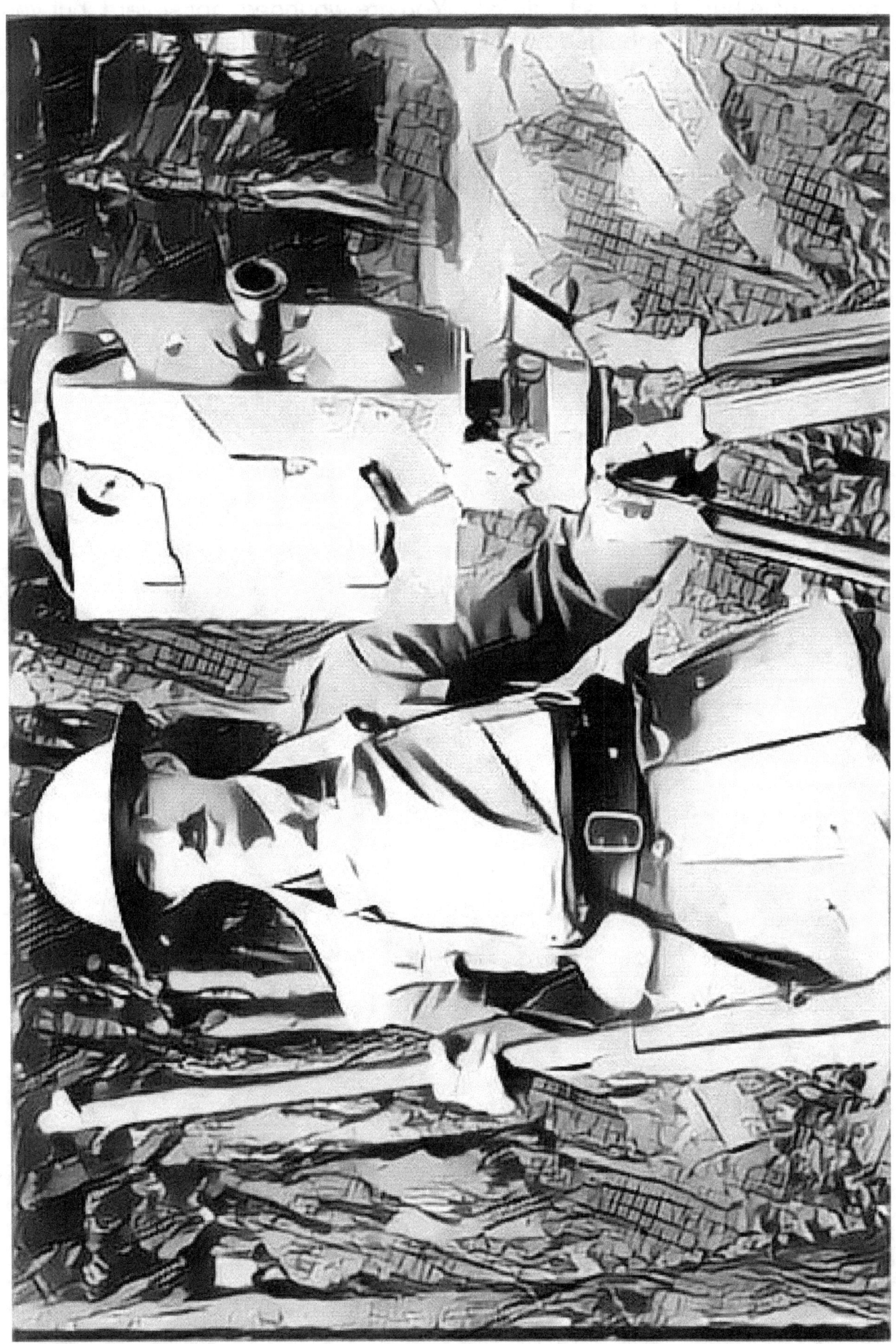

You are coming back from the battlefield. You are wounded, not severe, but your spirit it is totally broken by the shadows of war. Describe your feelings (use the image).

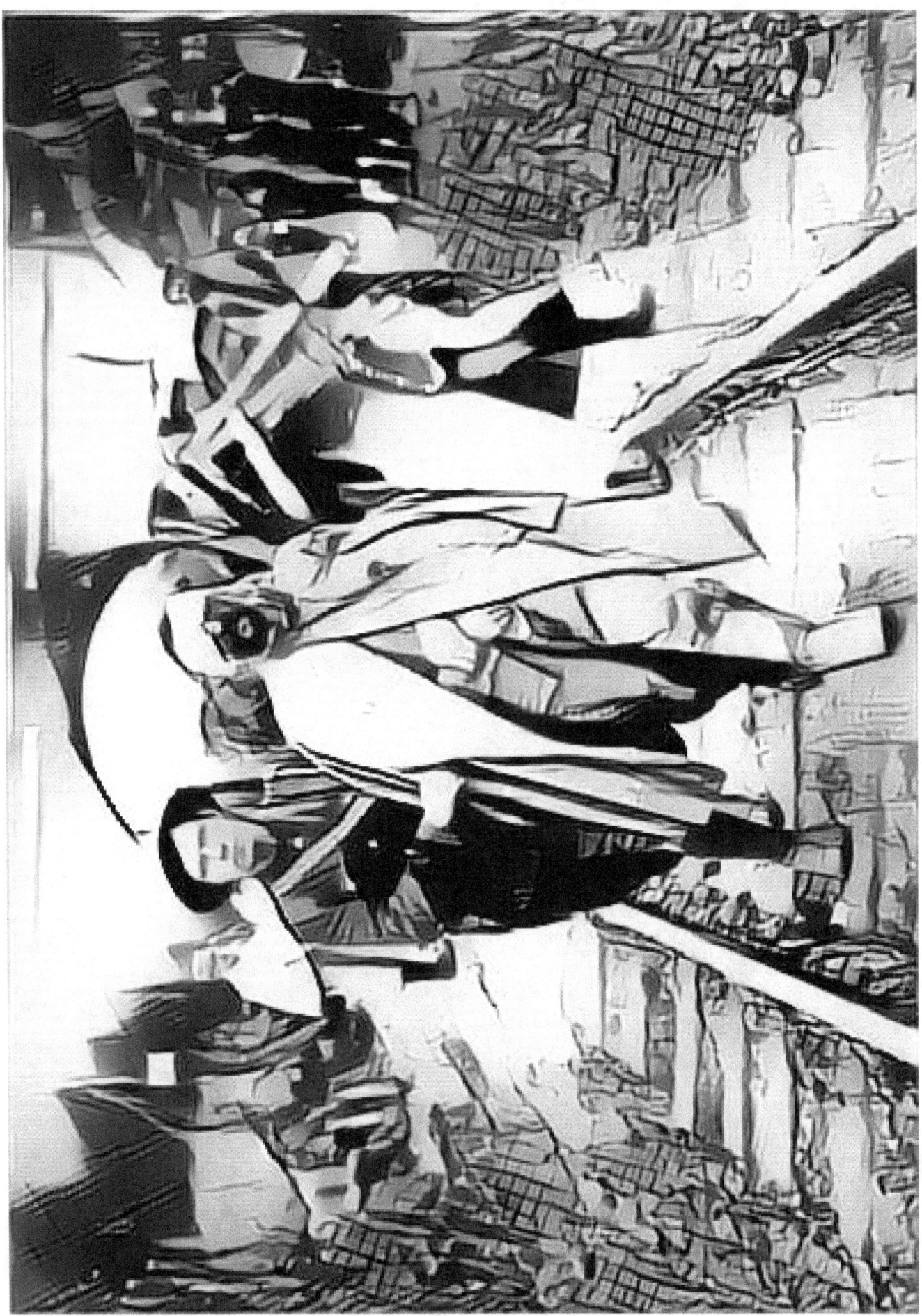

Women took over many traditionally male jobs and showed that they could perform them just as well as men.

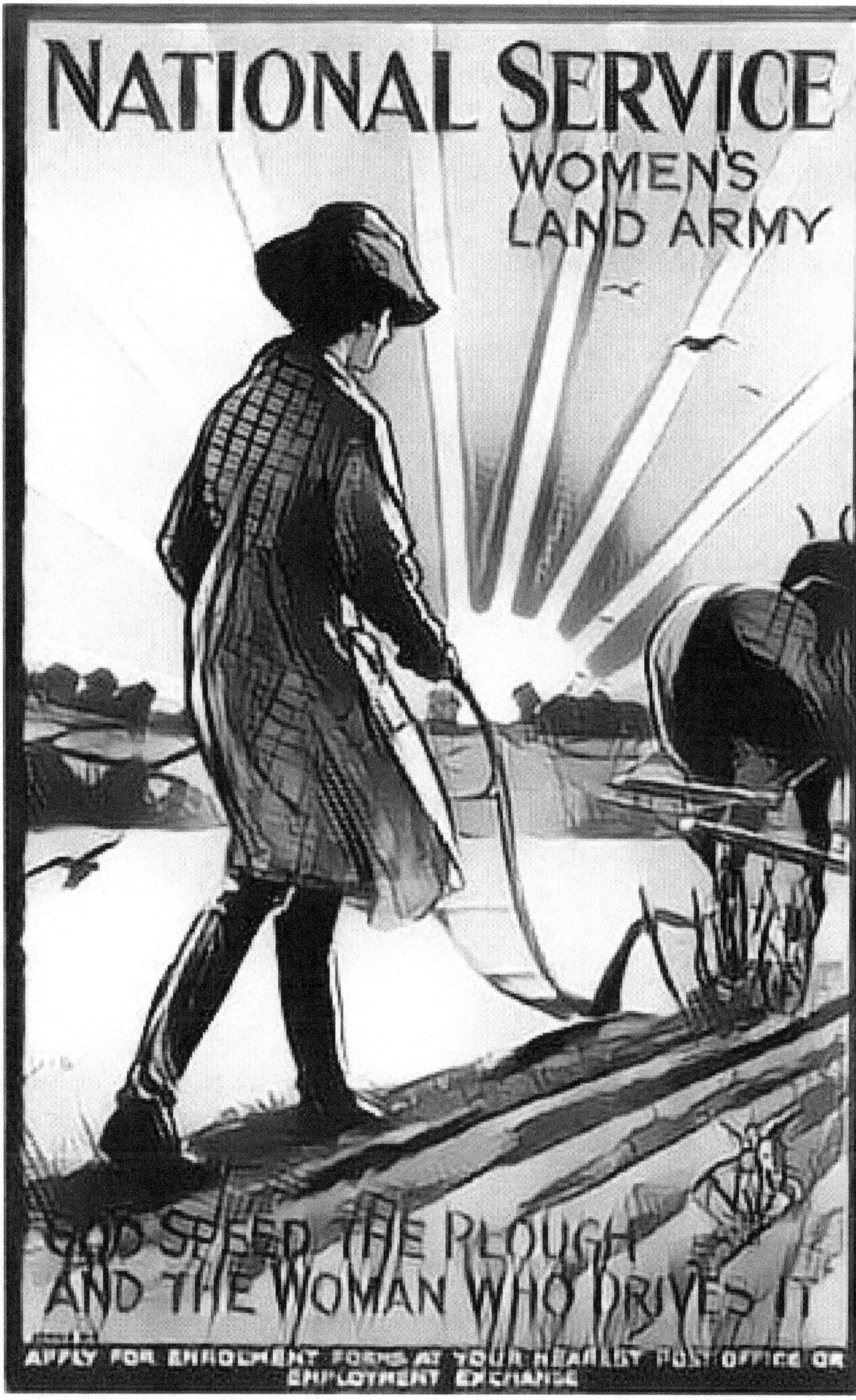
NATIONAL SERVICE
WOMEN'S
LAND ARMY
GOD SPEED THE PLOUGH
AND THE WOMAN WHO DRIVES IT
APPLY FOR ENROLMENT FORMS AT YOUR NEAREST POST OFFICE OR
EMPLOYMENT EXCHANGE

Early 1918, meat, sugar and fat were rationed products, as a fair way to allocate food and other scarce resources amongst the population. So this WW1 poster urges the people to save bread and not to waste food. The purpose was to loosen the U-boats stranglehold on WW1 Britain and in the long run help a positive outcome of the war.

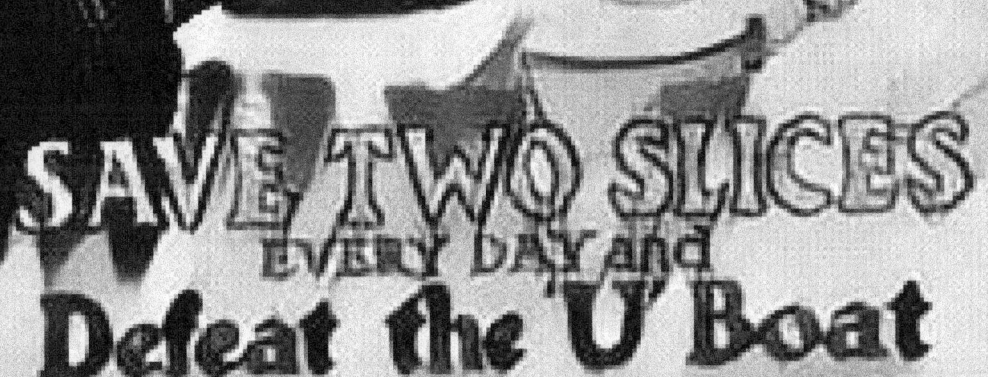

What would you do for your family? for your freedom? Describe what you have thought about this topic. Maybe it's a good idea to have a plan.

FOR YOUR BOY

Y.M.C.A

UNITED WAR WORK CAMPAIGN
NOVEMBER 11-18, 1918

What can you do to help your country? What can you do to help your family, your neighbors or your community?

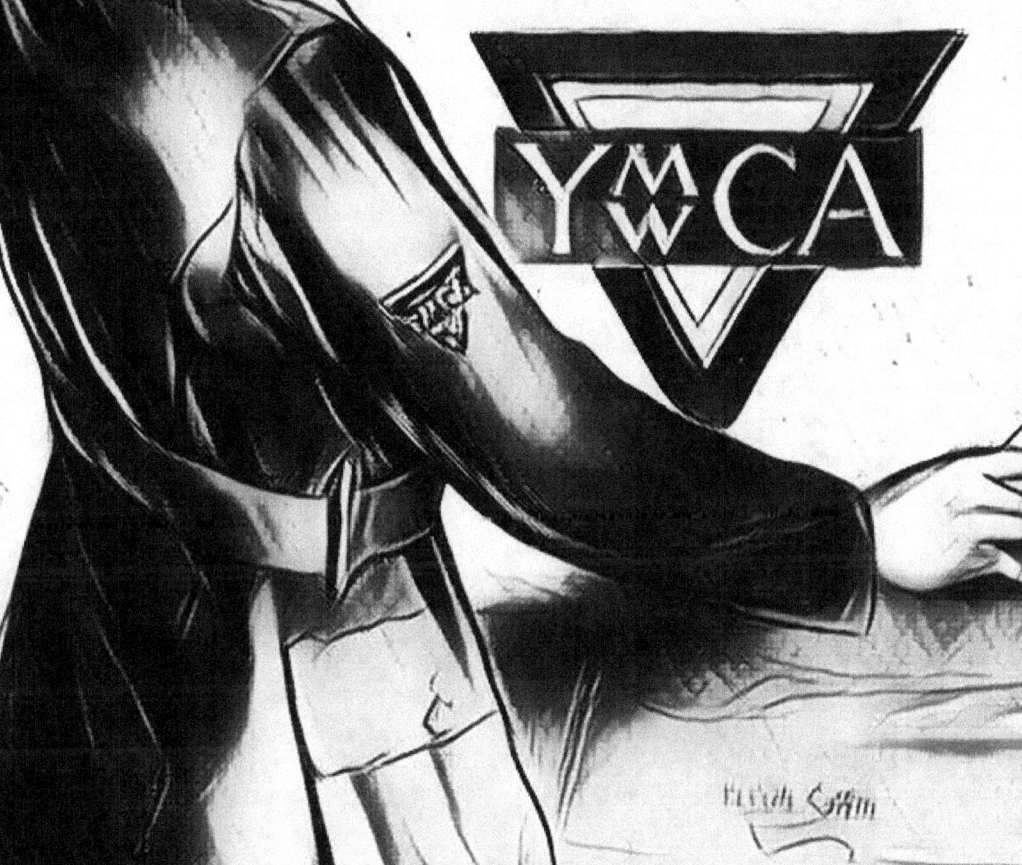

The Battle of Belleau Wood (1–26 June 1918) occurred during the German Spring Offensive in World War I, near the Marne River in France. The battle was fought between the U.S. 2nd (under the command of Major General Omar Bundy) and 3rd Divisions along with French and British forces against an assortment of German units including elements from the 237th, 10th, 197th, 87th, and 28th Divisions. The battle has become a key component of the lore of the United States Marine Corps.

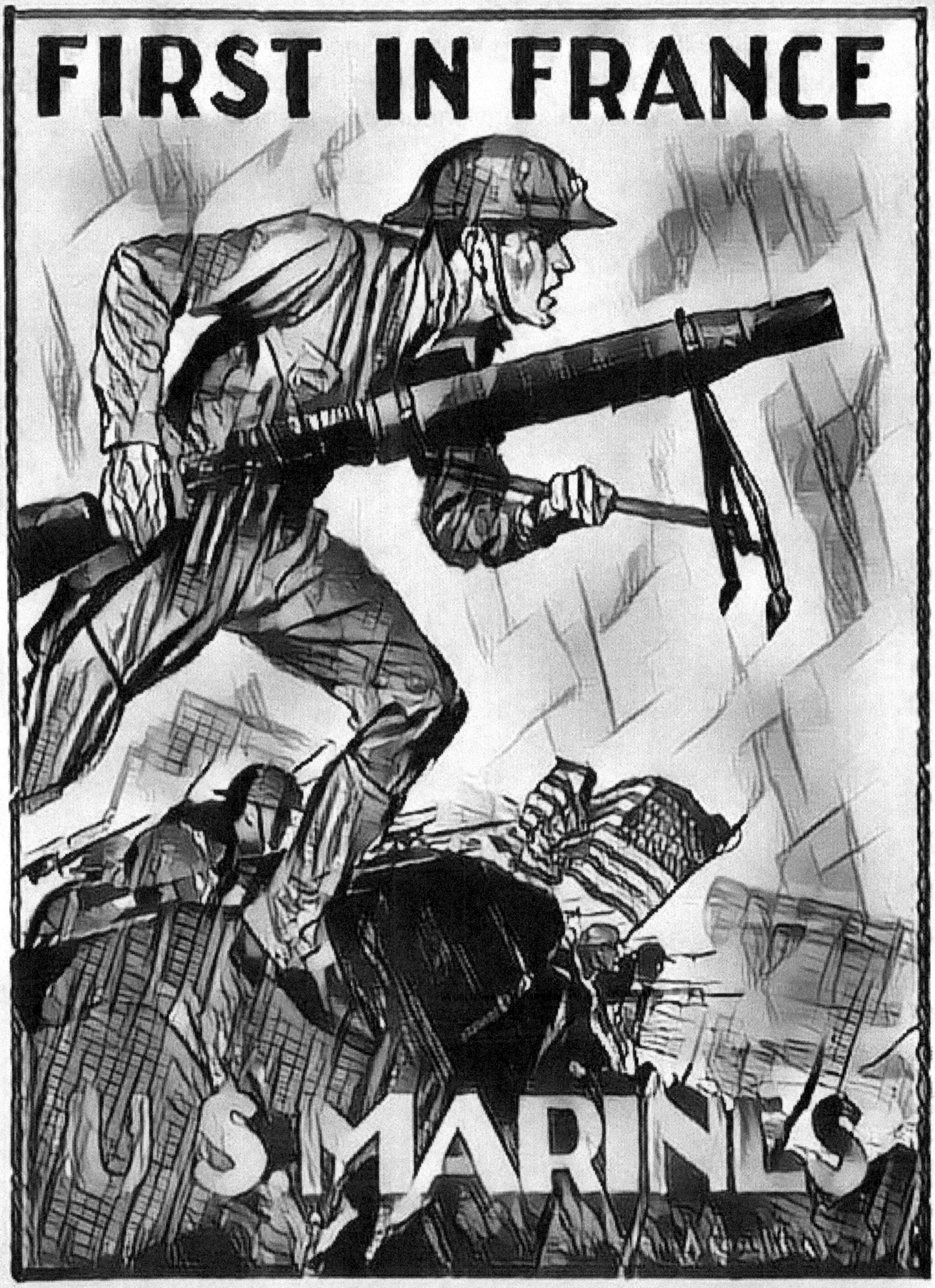
FIRST IN FRANCE
U.S. MARINES

"It's a Long Way to Tipperary" is a British music hall song written by Jack Judge and co-credited to Henry James "Harry" Williams. It was allegedly written for a 5-shilling bet in Stalybridge on 30 January 1912 and performed the next night at the local music hall. Now commonly called "It's a Long Way to Tipperary", the original printed music calls it "It's a Long, Long Way to Tipperary." It became popular among soldiers in the First World War and is remembered as a song of that war.

THE SONG THEY SING
AS THEY MARCH ALONG

TOMMY ATKINS

IT'S A
LONG, LONG
WAY TO
TIPPERARY

WRITTEN AND COMPOSED BY
JACK JUDGE
AND
HARRY WILLIAMS

Price 60 Cents

For the United States of America and Canada
CHAPPELL & CO. LTD.
41 EAST 34th STREET   347 YONGE STREET
NEW YORK   TORONTO

What´s the story on this picture?

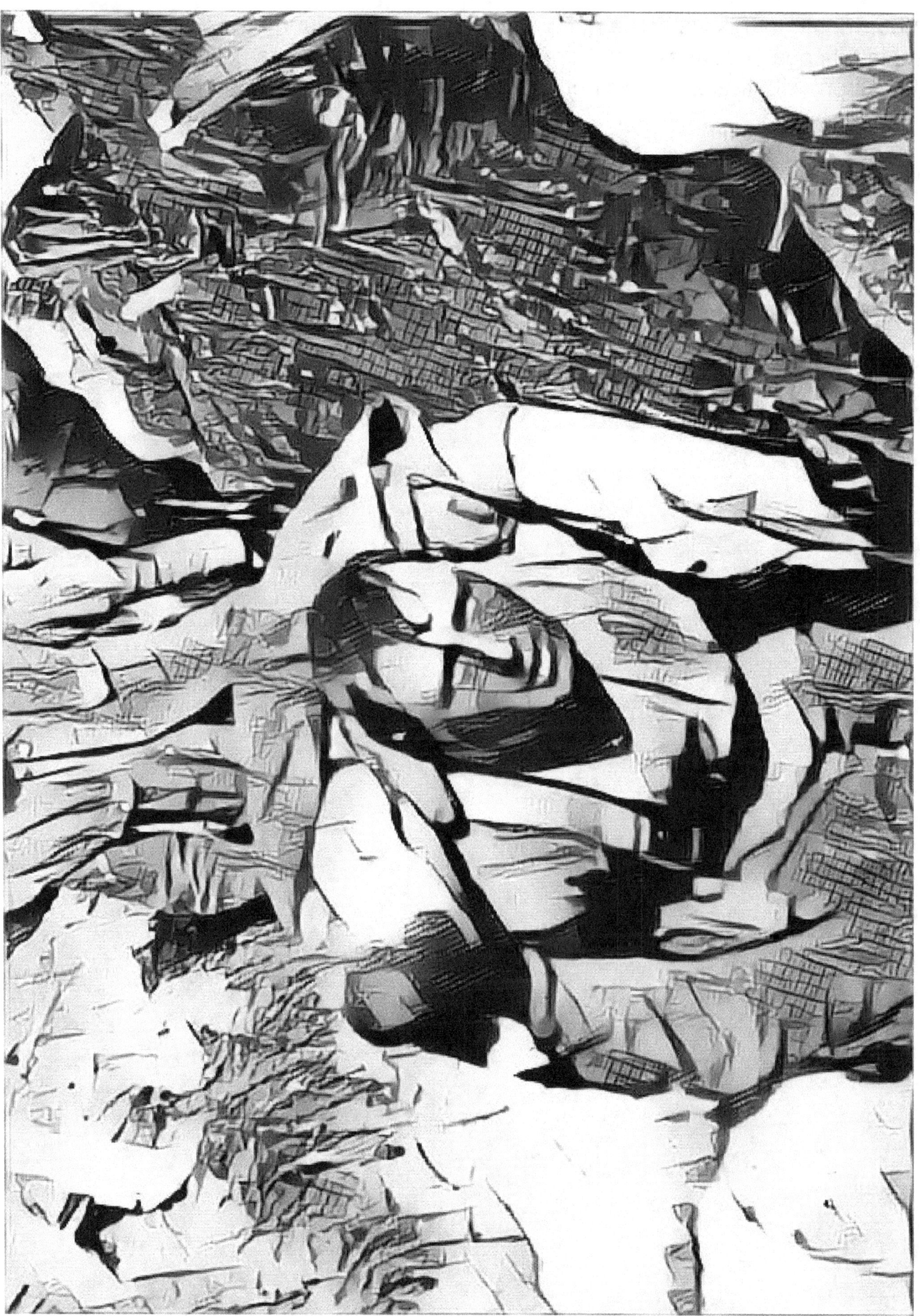

"Your money or his life." Like many posters produced during the war, the imagery and text in this poster contrasts and draws a parallel between the heroic sacrifices of those at the front with the un-heroic but important act of contributing money to the war effort.

YOUR MONEY OR HIS LIFE

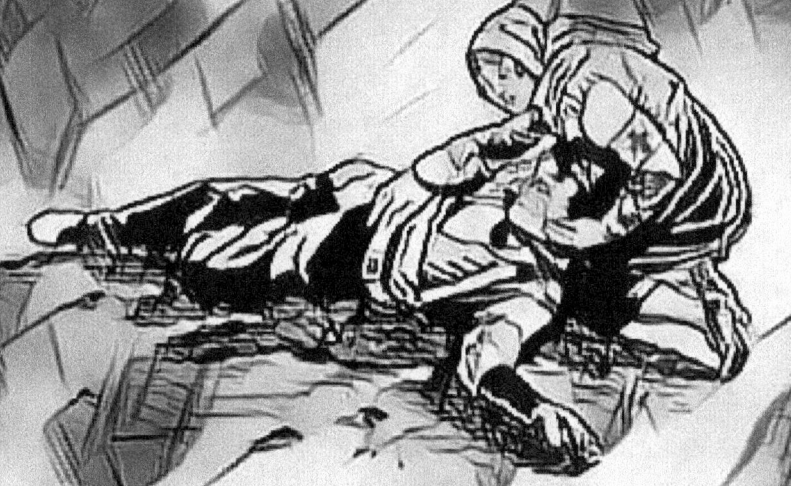

SUBSCRIBE TO THE WAR FUND
RED CROSS WEEK
JUNE 18TH TO 25TH

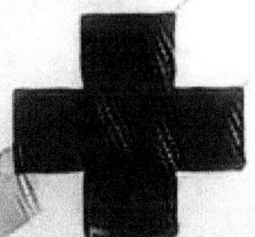

COMMITTEE ON PUBLIC SAFETY
STATE OF NEW HAMPSHIRE

Poster showing a German soldier crushed by a monumental coin. LOC Notes: Poster no. 23. Date Created/Published: London : Parliamentary War Savings Committee, 1915.

LEND YOUR FIVE SHILLINGS TO YOUR COUNTRY AND

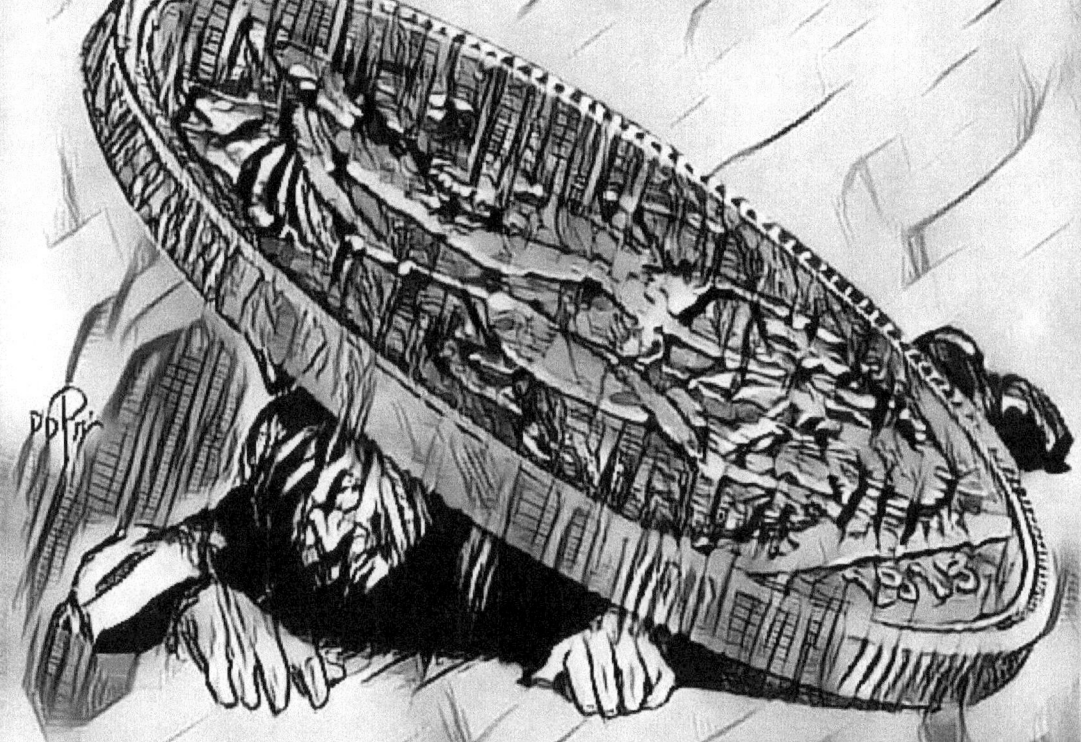

CRUSH THE GERMANS

PUBLISHED BY THE PARLIAMENTARY WAR SAVINGS COMMITTEE LONDON POSTER N°18   PRINTED BY DAVID ALLEN & SONS L⁴ HARROW WEALD / MIDDLESEX

Can you see what is inside that place? Share what you see drawing in this space.

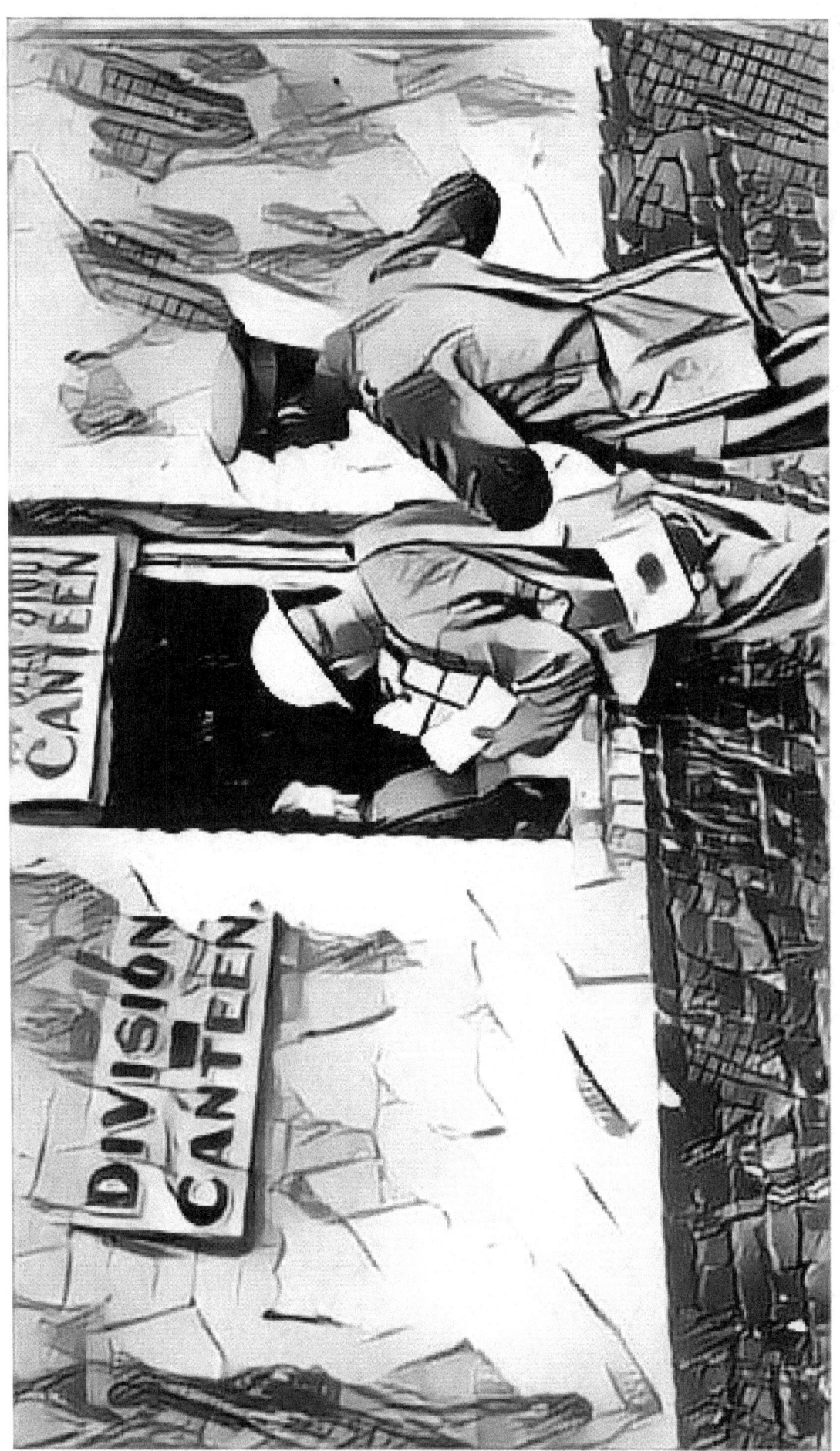

The First World War brought an end to one of the biggest periods of immigration in American history. During the decade leading up to the war, an average of 1 million immigrants per year arrived in the United States, with about three-quarters of them entering through the Ellis Island immigration station in New York Harbor.

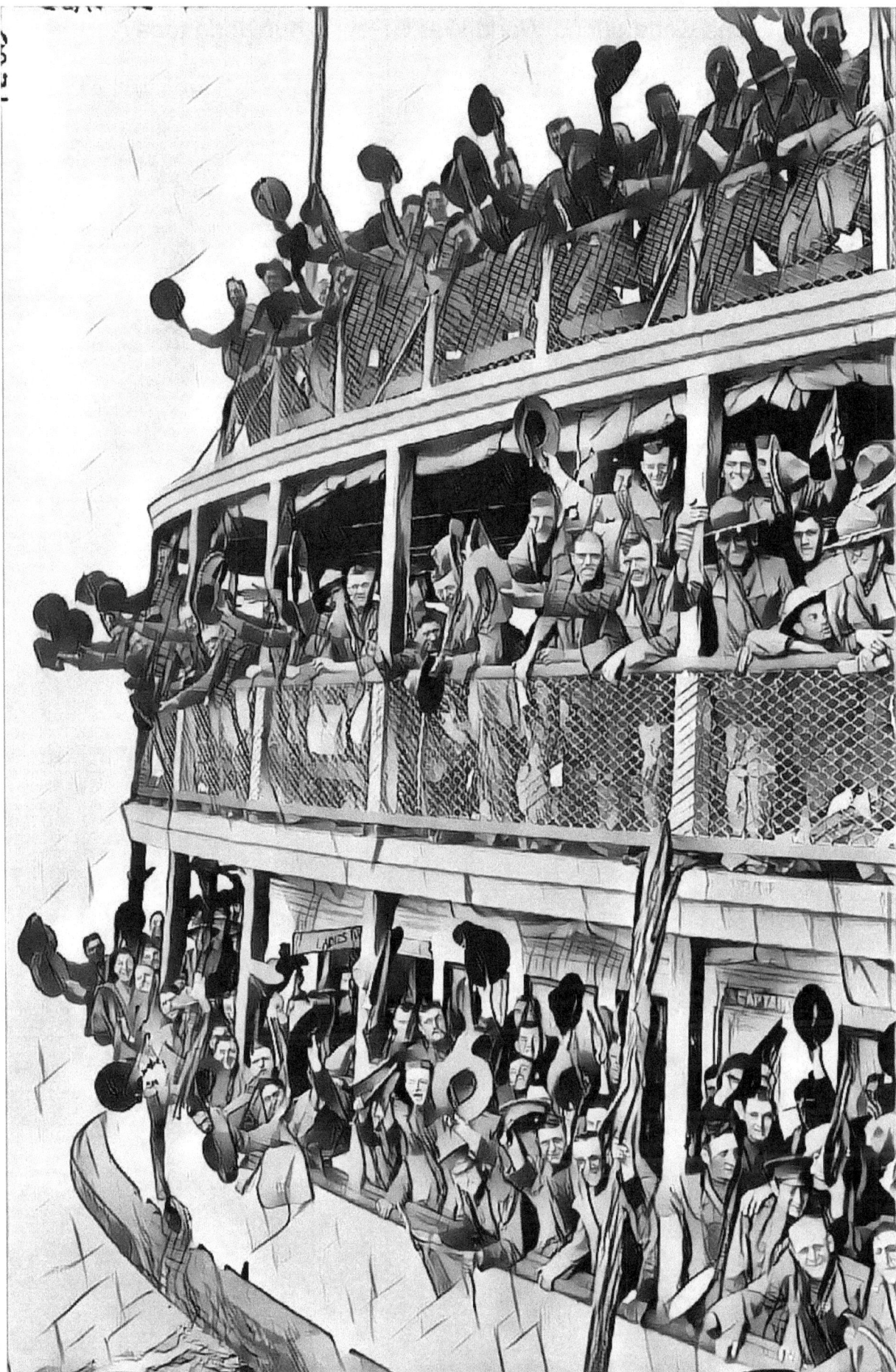

The world during World War I. How is our world today?

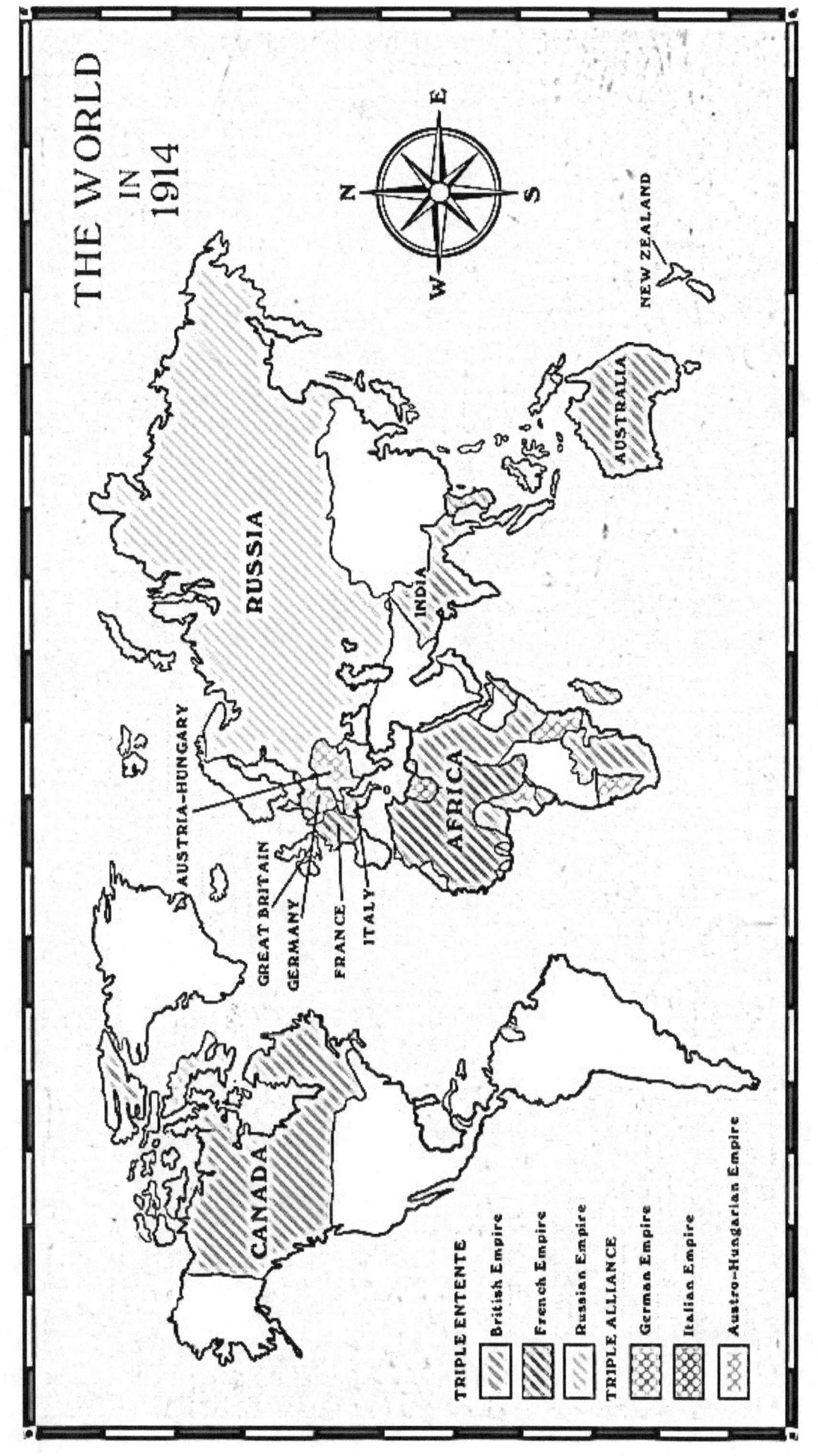

What are your thoughts about this image?

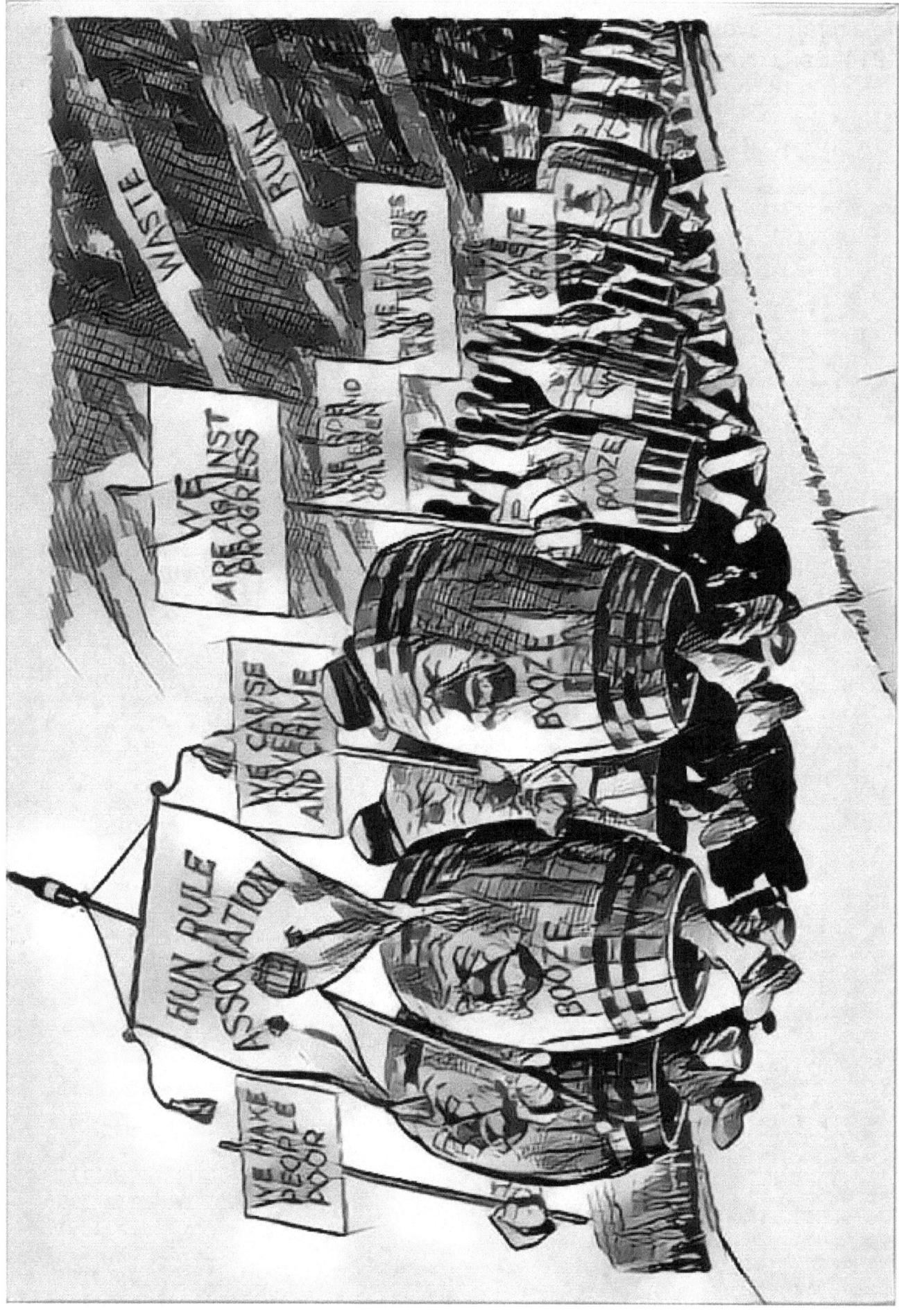

The aircraft played a pivotal role for all sides of World War I when the conflict began in 1914. Early forms were typically unarmed and used in the reconnaissance role until personal weapons were added.

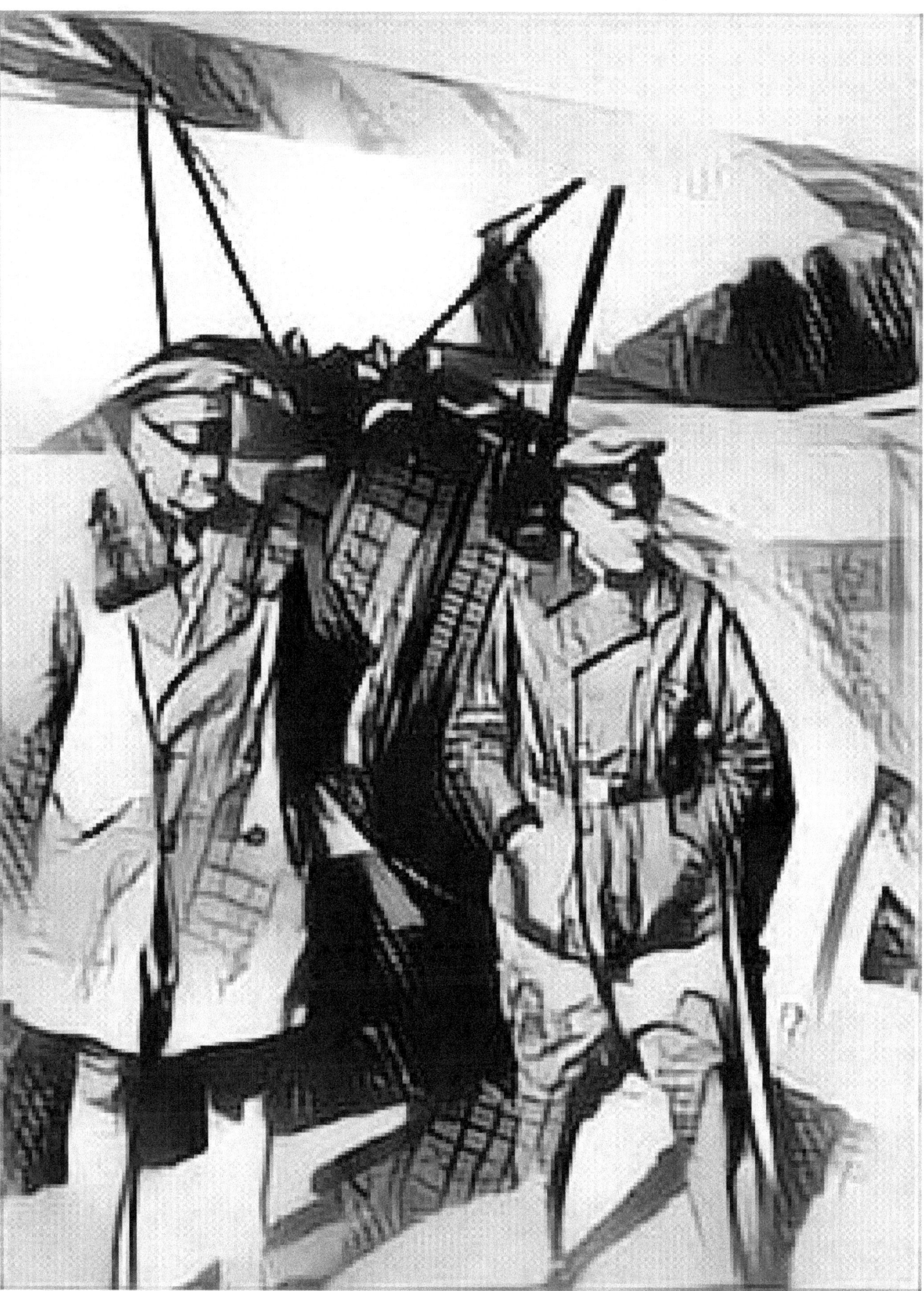

What do you think happened in this place?

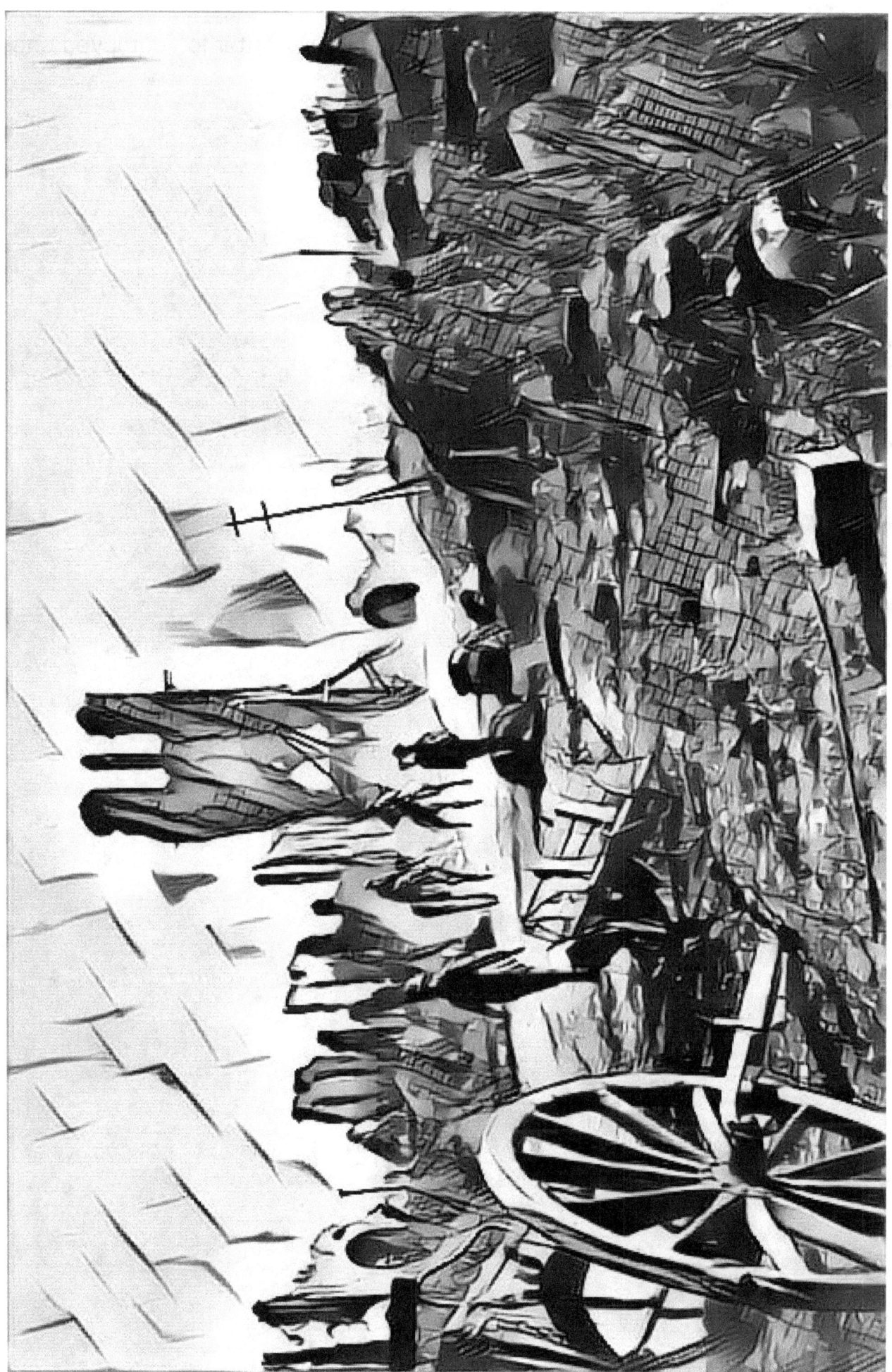

It's hard to say goodbye. Create and share a farewell letter to your loved ones.

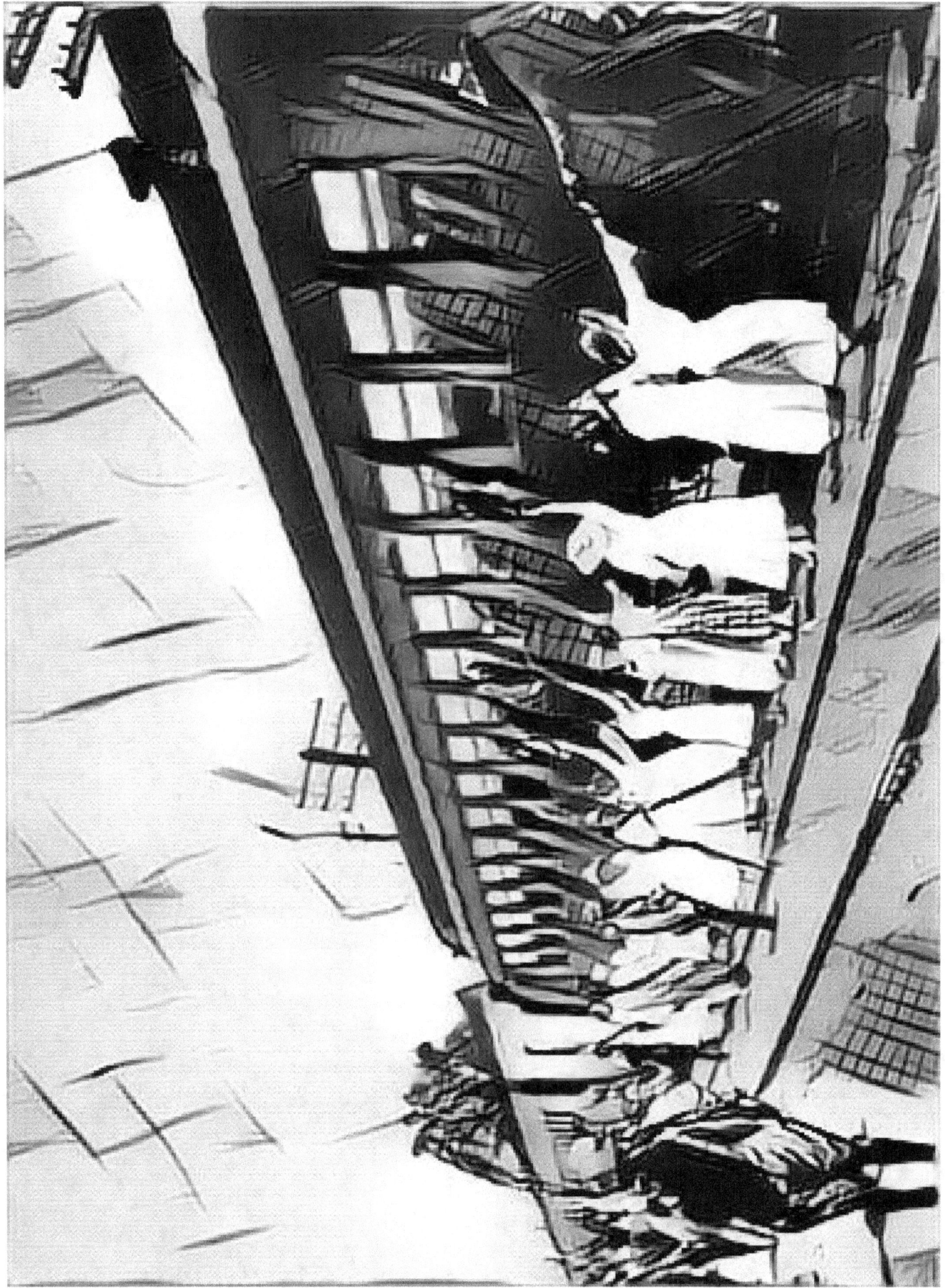

World War 1 fought using machine guns,tanks, early airplanes, and poisonous gas.

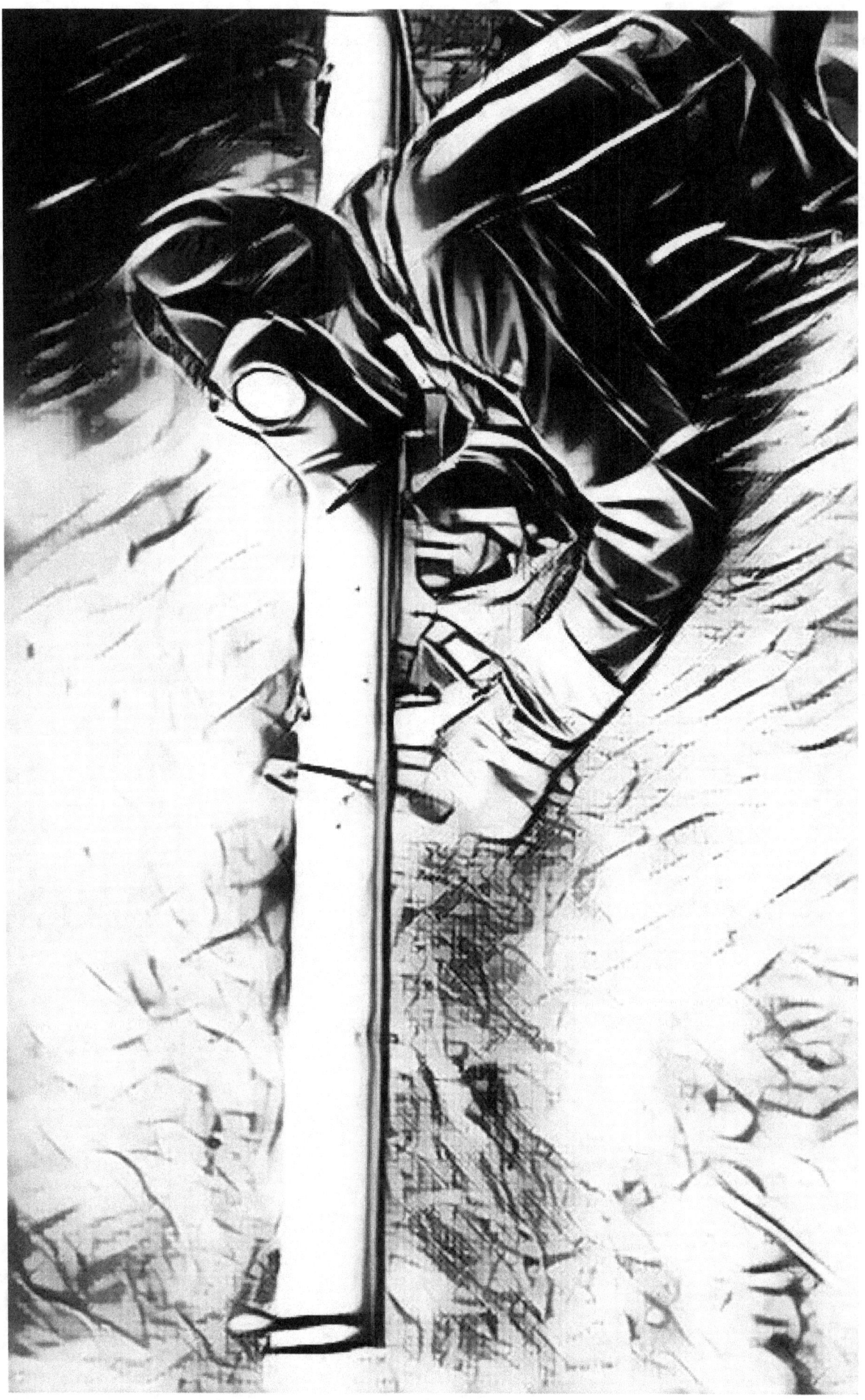

Different variations of prototypes of anti gas masks were created during war time.

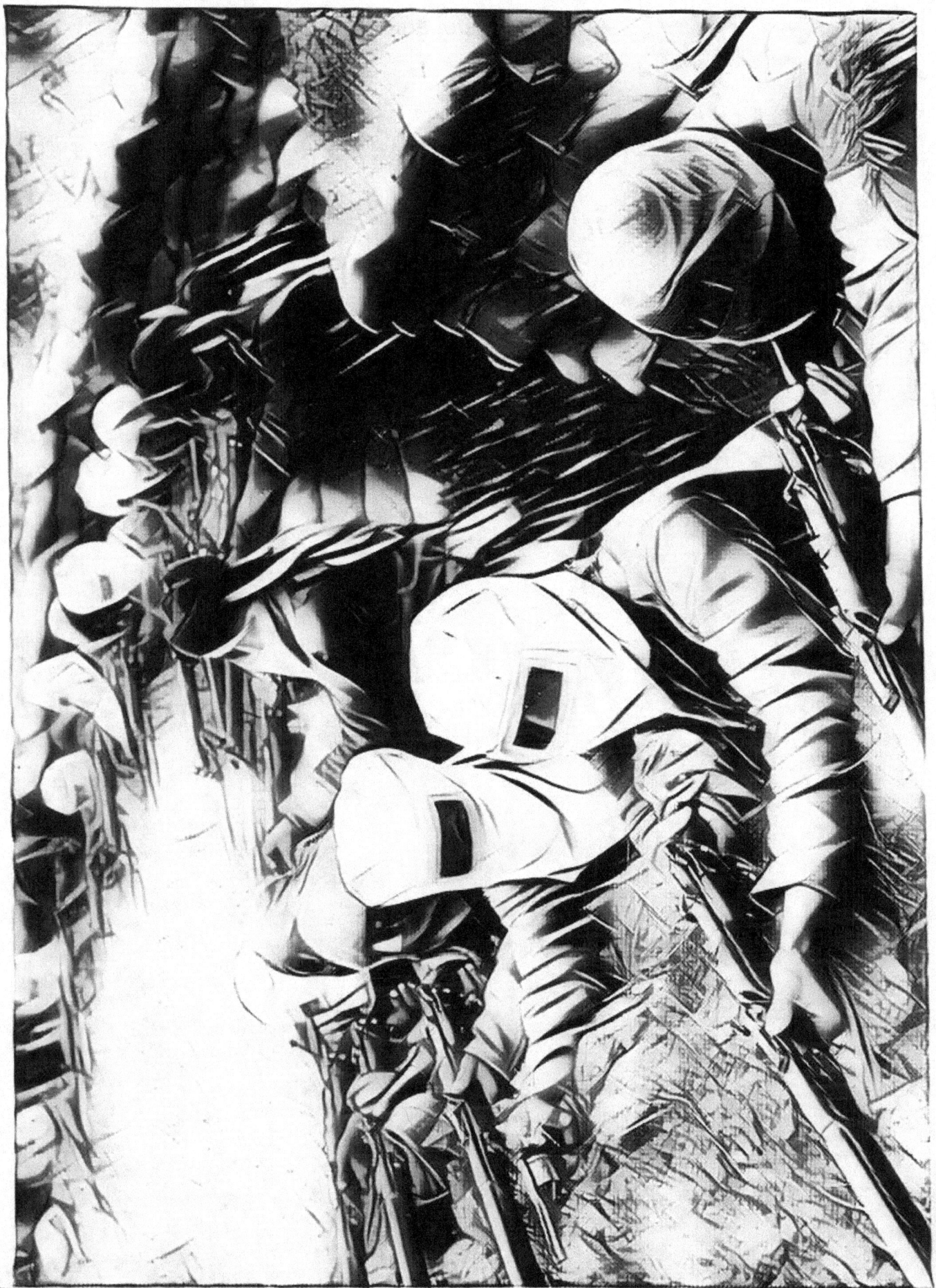

Another style of anti gas mask

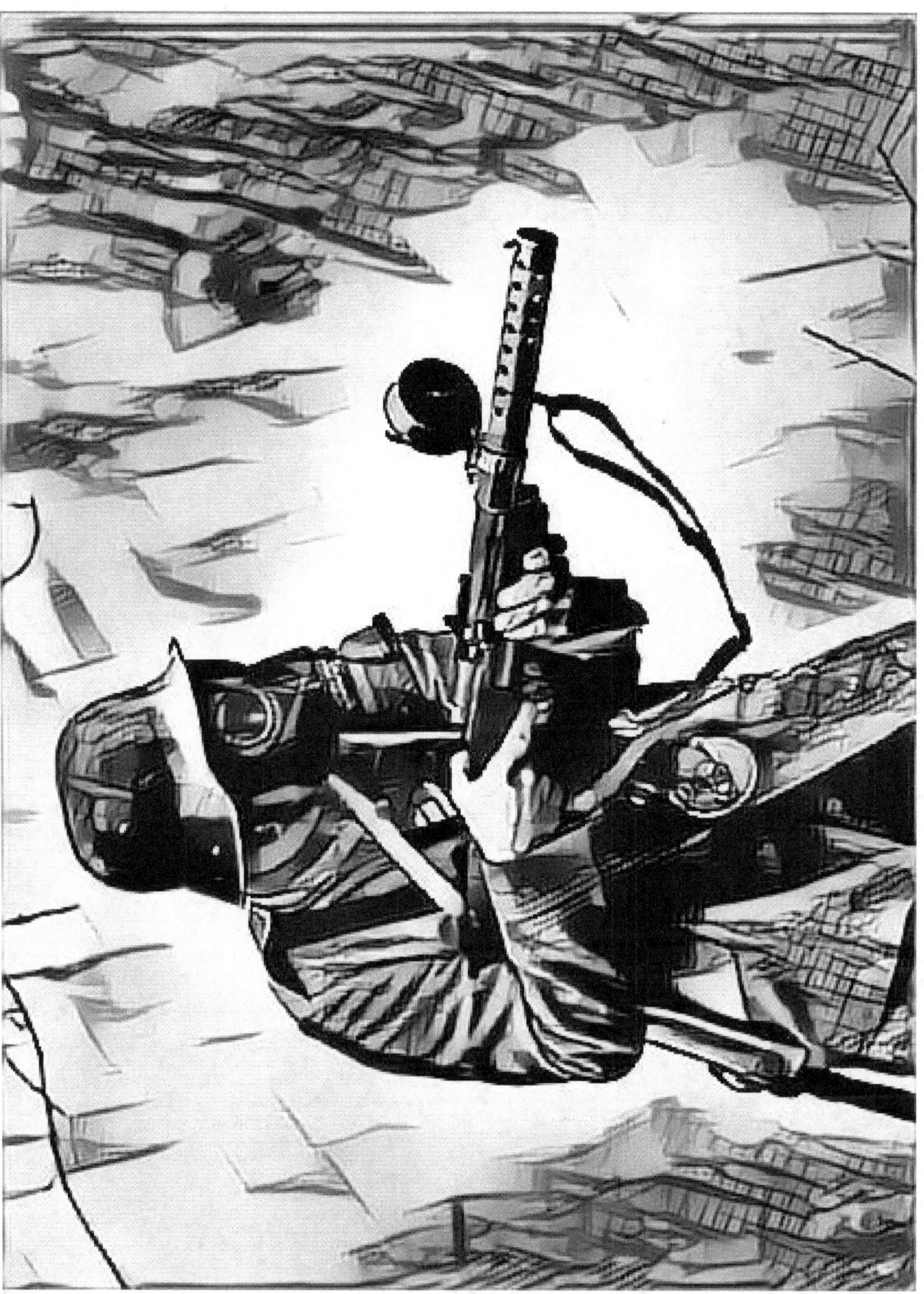

Getting everything ready for war.

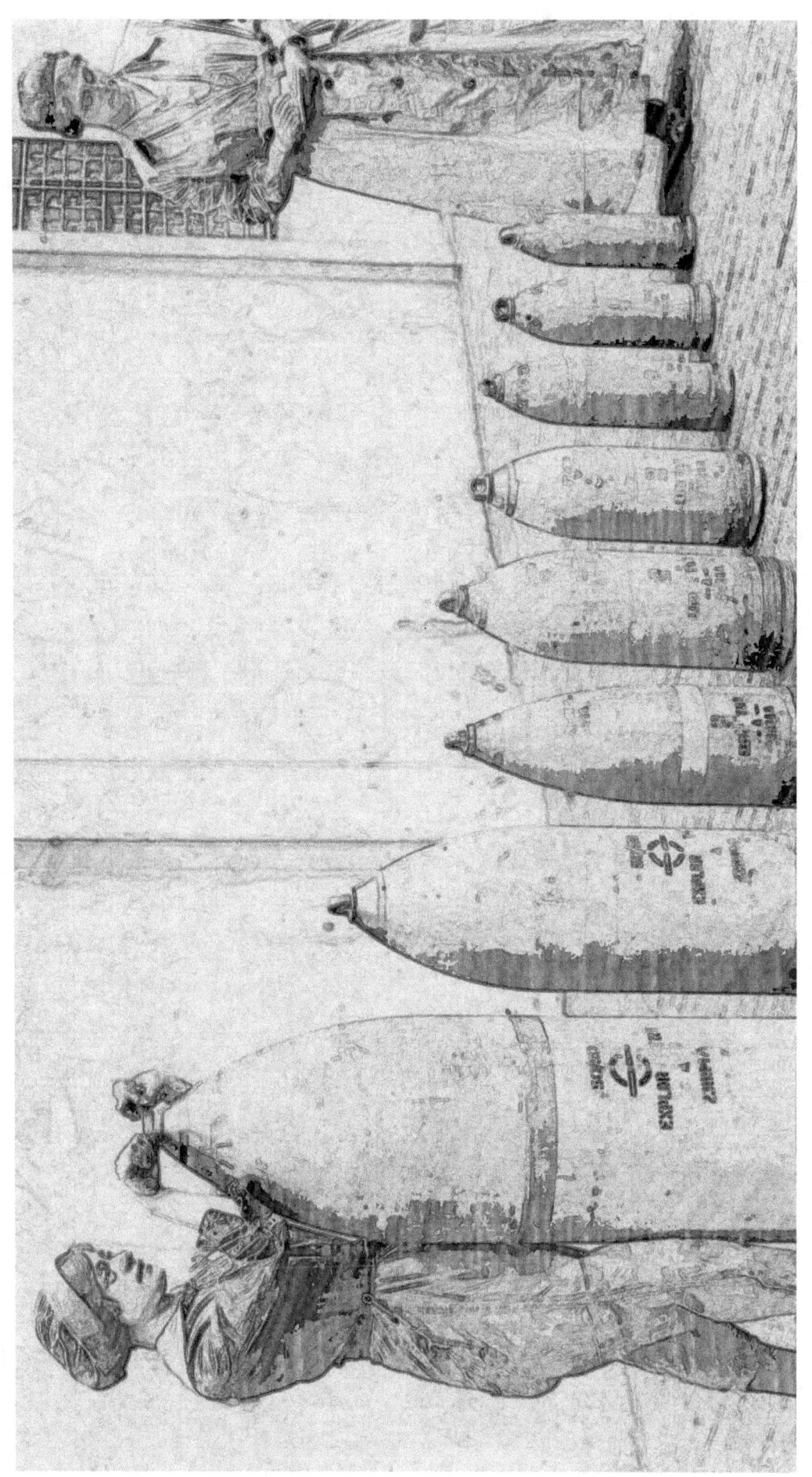

Peace!! It's something we all want but a few try to make it never be that way. Share your thoughts about this.

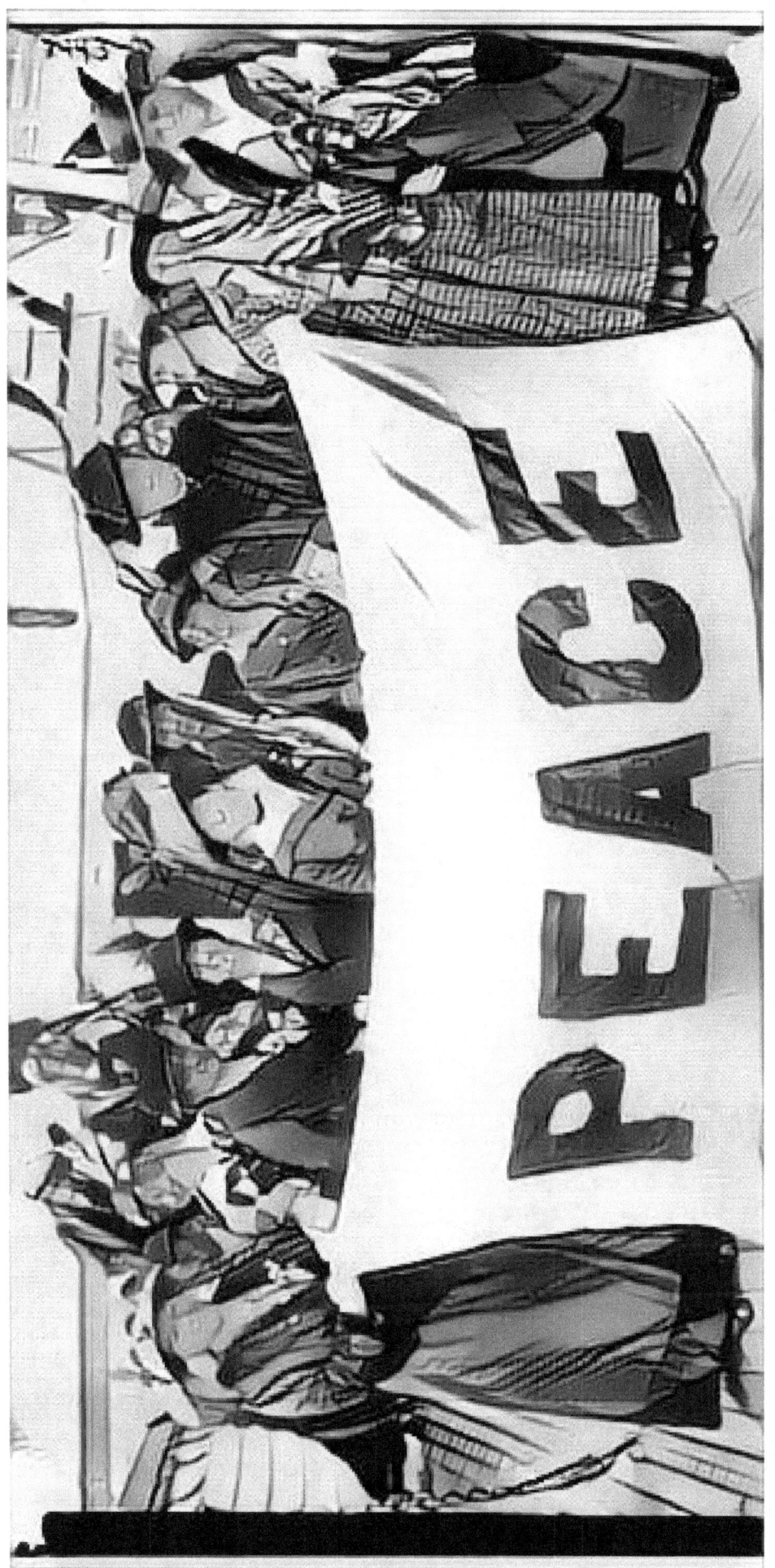

Ready for the fight? How prepared are you in case something bad happens? Do you have any plans?

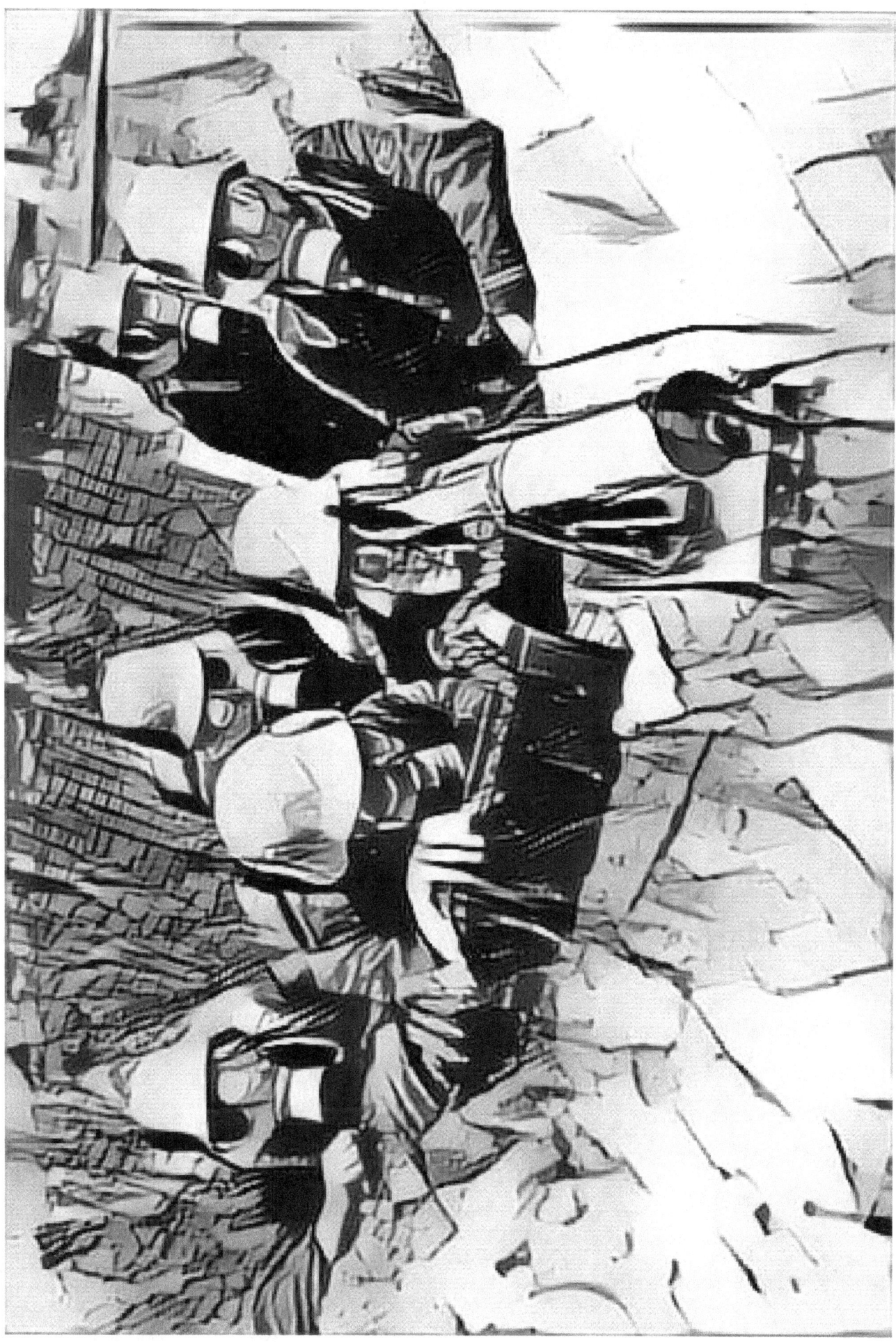

Create a short story for this US Forces. Be creative.

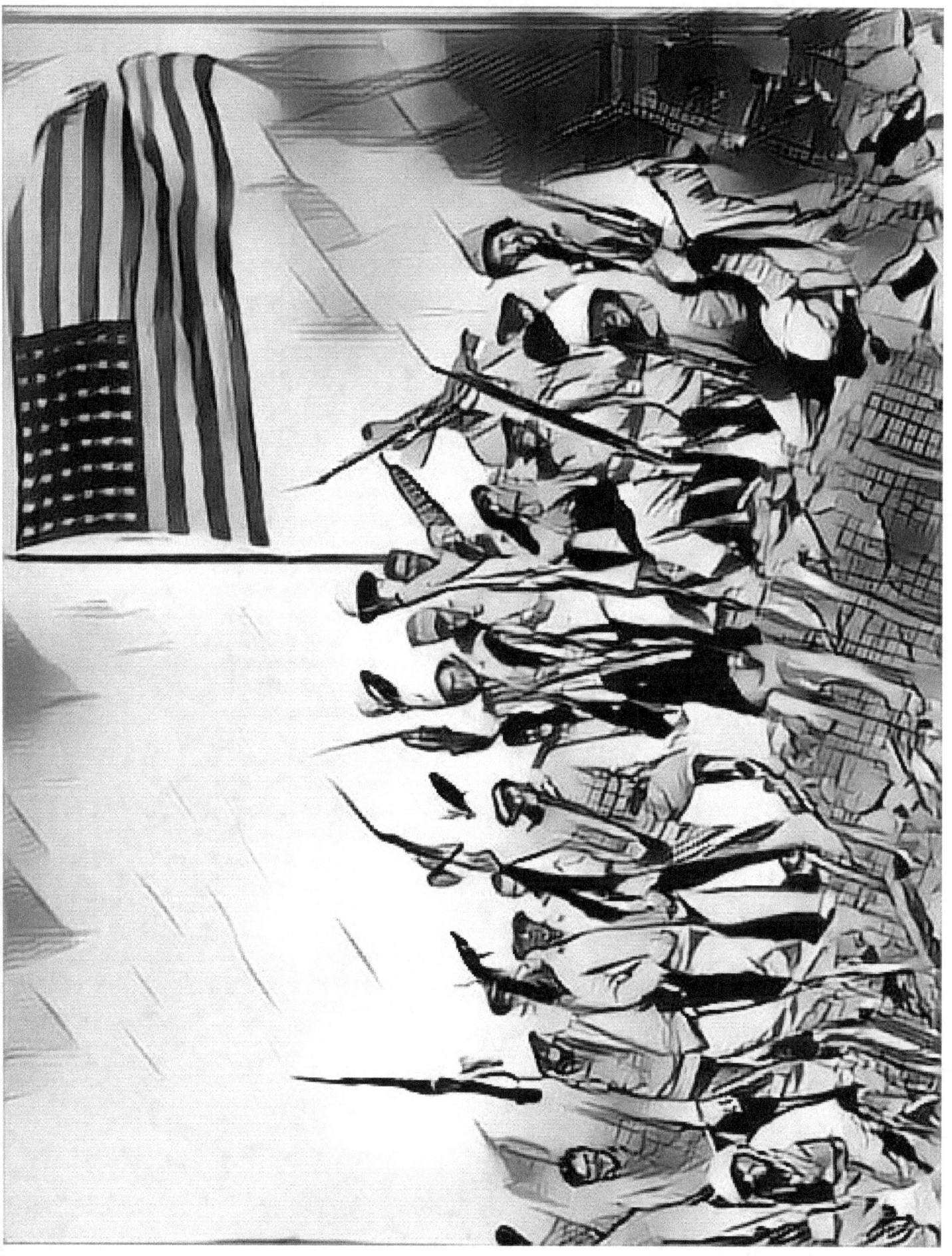

Free notes.

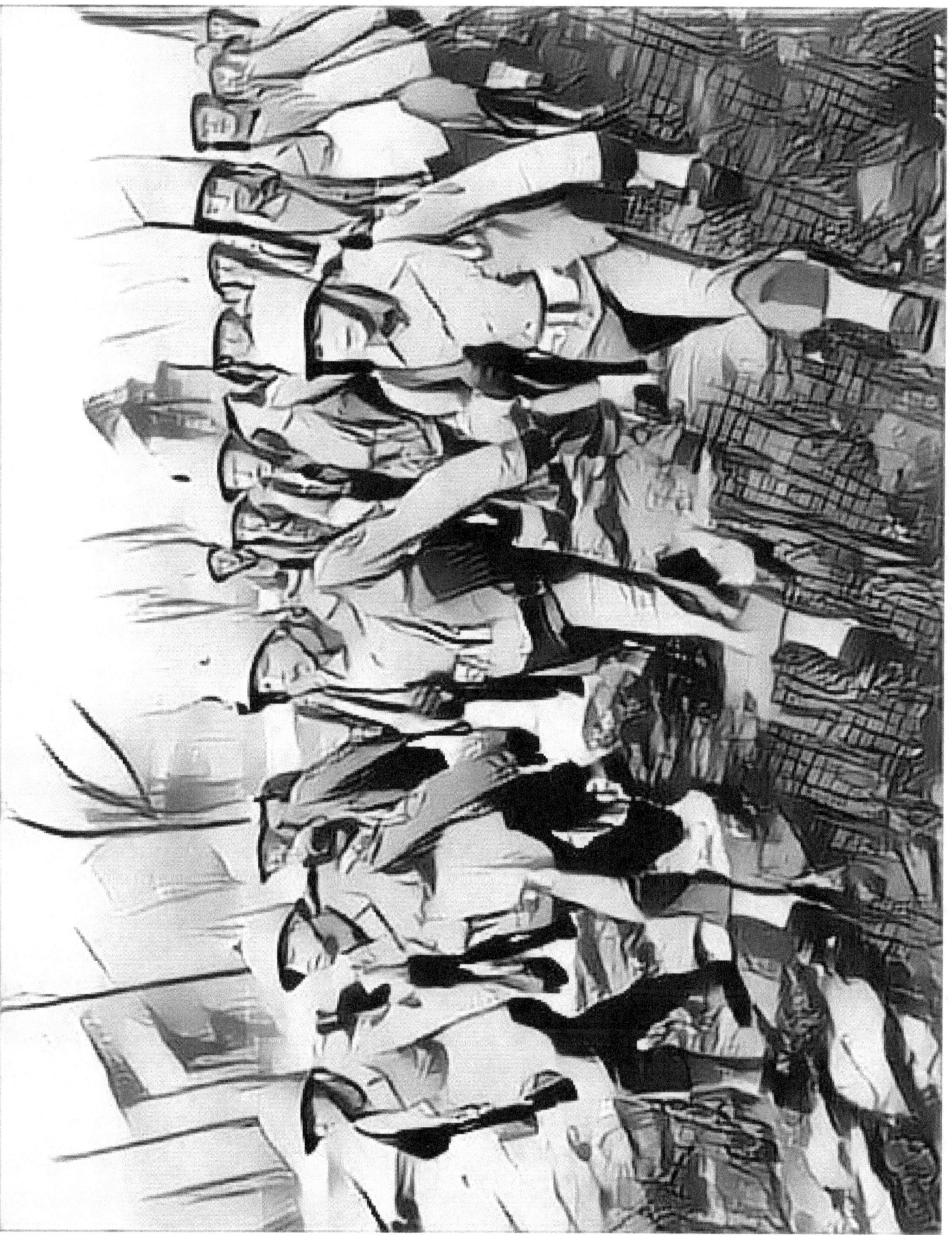

Free notes.

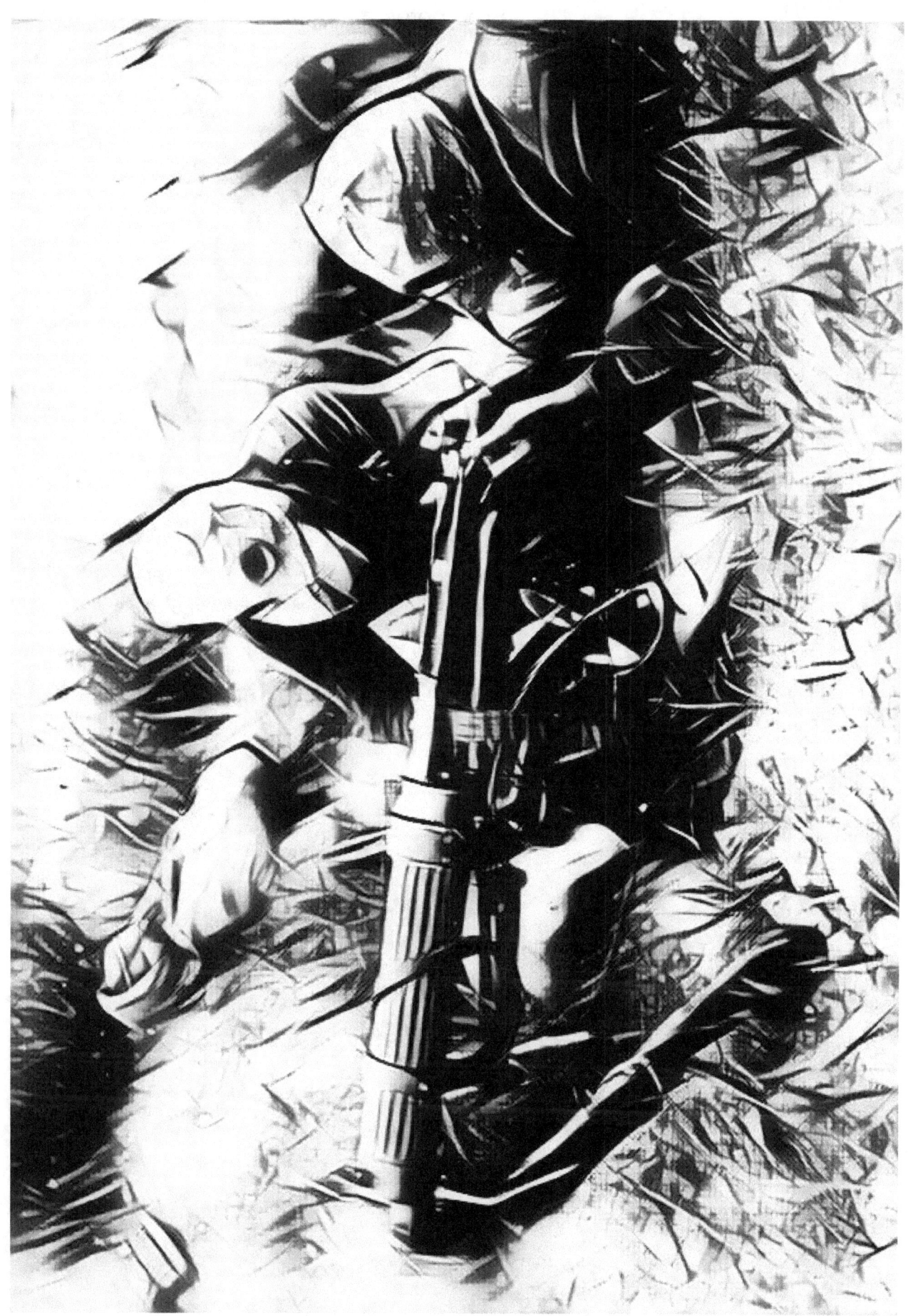

Free notes.

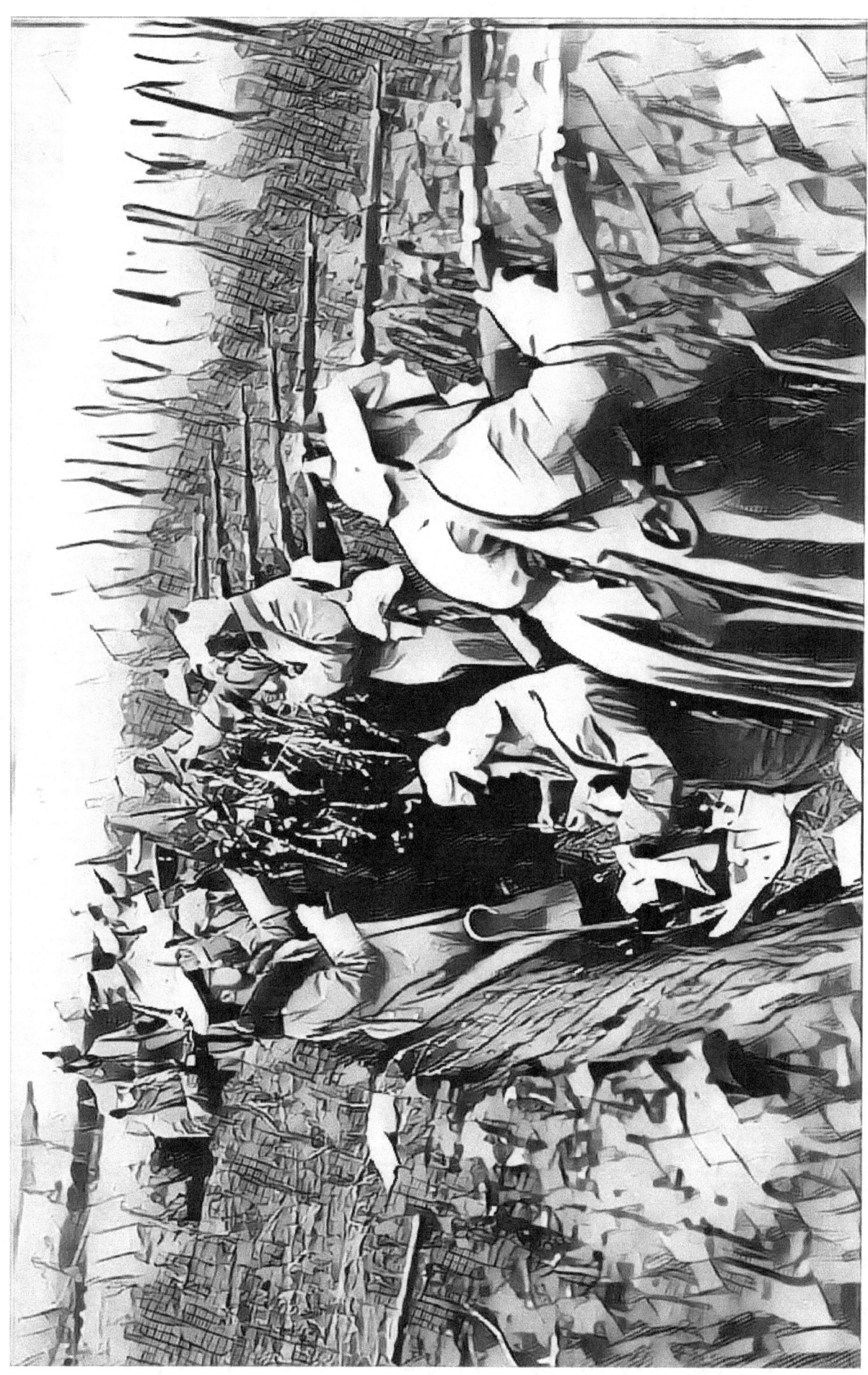

Free notes.

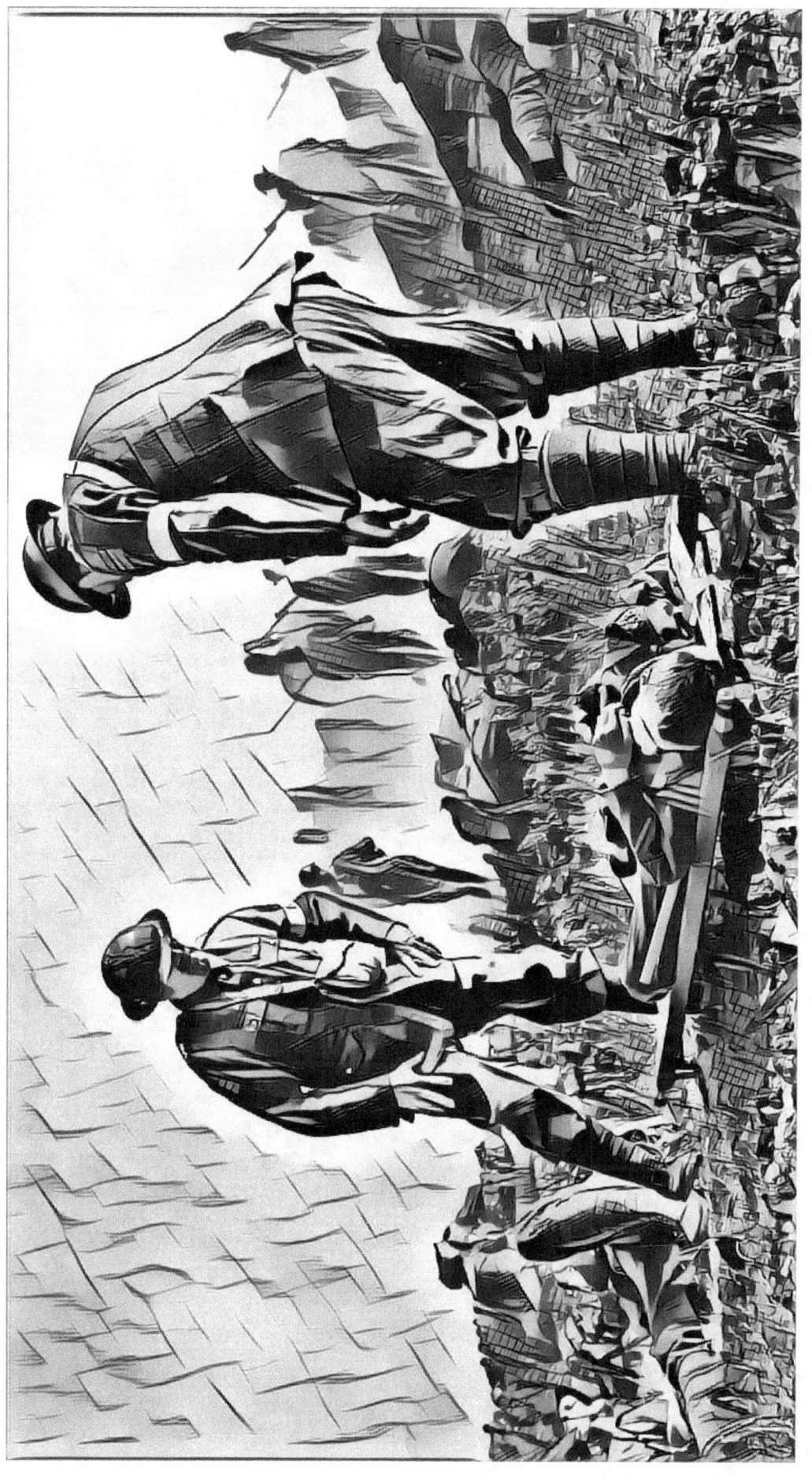

Free notes.

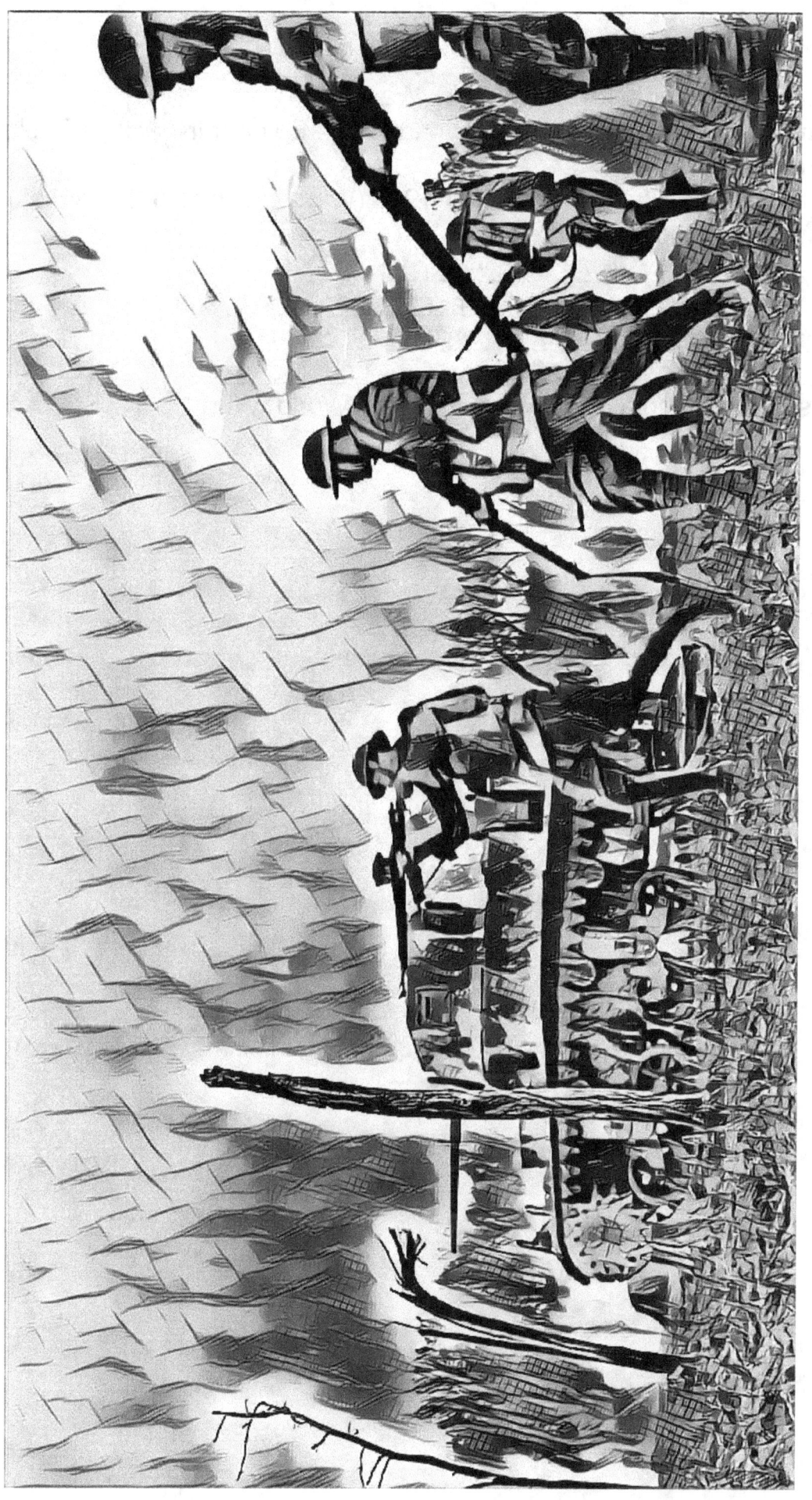

References

1. https://en.wikipedia.org/wiki/World_War_I
2. Hamilton, John C. Weapons of World War I. Edina, MN: ABDO Publishing Company, 2004.
3. Turner, Jason. World War I: 1914-1918 (Wars Day by Day). Mankato, MN: Brown Bear Books, 2008.
4. https://www.factretriever.com/world-war-i-facts
5. https://www.nps.gov/articles/immigration-and-the-great-war.htm
6. https://www.emaze.com/@AQIQWZW
7. https://en.wikipedia.org/wiki/Lists_of_World_War_I_topics
8. https://en.wikipedia.org/wiki/Timeline_of_World_War_I

ABOUT THIS BOOK

This book is intended to remind us how terrible and devastating war is. countries in ruins, people with great sadness in their souls. collapsed economies and misery everywhere.

NO MORE WARS!!

WORLD WAR I
ADULT COLORING BOOK
REAL LIFE IMAGES

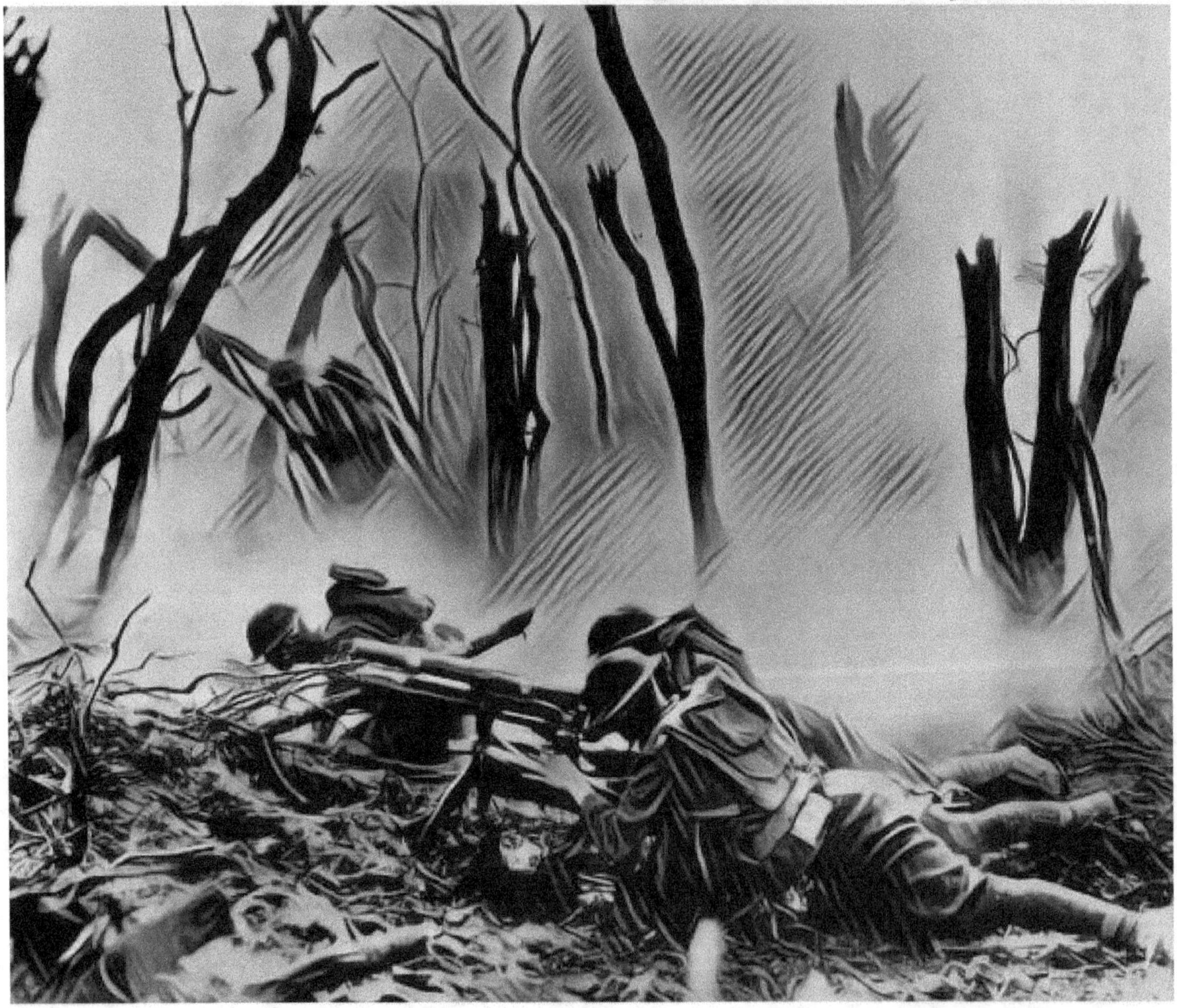

MDS
Publishing Company

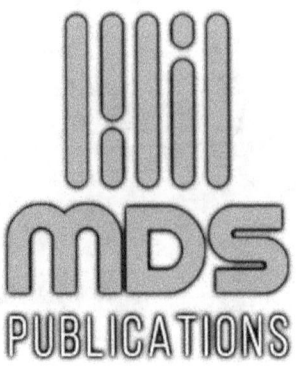